FINANCIAL GROWTH STRATEGIST JOURNAL:

WEALTH, GOALS, AND SMARTER DECISIONS

NIGEL PICKERTON

DISCLAIMER

The information provided in this book is intended solely for educational purposes and should not be construed as financial or investment advice. The content is not a recommendation to buy, sell, or hold any stocks, securities, or other financial instruments. The strategies and opinions expressed are based on the author's personal experience and research; however, investing in the stock market carries inherent risks, and past performance does not guarantee future results.

Readers are strongly advised to conduct their own research or seek advice from a licensed financial professional before making any investment decisions. The author and publisher are not responsible for any financial losses or gains that may result from the use of this material. Investing involves risks, including the potential loss of principal, and it is important to assess your individual financial situation and risk tolerance.

This book does not cover all possible risks or scenarios associated with stock trading, and market conditions can change rapidly. Always consult with a qualified advisor before entering into any financial transactions.

Financial Growth Strategist Journal: Wealth, Goals, and Smarter Decisions

Published by Taida Publishing
www.taidapublishing.com

ISBN: 979-8-89214-120-8

Edition: First Edition

Disclaimer:
The information provided in this book is for general informational and educational purposes only and is not a substitute for professional financial advice. The author and publisher are not liable for any losses or damages related to actions or failures to act related to the content of this book. Readers should consult a licensed financial advisor before making any financial decisions.

Opinions Expressed:
The views and opinions expressed in this book are solely those of the author and do not necessarily reflect the official policy or position of TAIDA PUBLISHING.

Credits:
Cover Illustration by Leon Lendowski
Edited by Peter Michael Wolfe

TABLE OF CONTENTS

01 COMPREHENSIVE GUIDE TO STOCK TRADING STRATEGIES

This section outlines a structured approach to stock trading, integrating both fundamental and technical analysis, market sentiment evaluation, risk management, and psychological preparedness. It serves as a roadmap for traders looking to enhance their decision-making processes and improve their overall trading performance.

Start with Conviction

Combine Fundamental and Technical Analysis

- **Fundamental Analysis**
  - Identify Good Companies Blessed by the Market
  - Analyze Company's Financial Health
  - Consider Global Macroeconomic Events
  - Pay Attention to Company News and Reactions
- **Technical Analysis**
  - Look for Relative Linearity in Stock Trends
  - Analyze Support and Resistance Levels
  - Monitor Stock's Response to Key Price Levels
  - Use Technical Indicators: Moving Averages, RSI, MACD

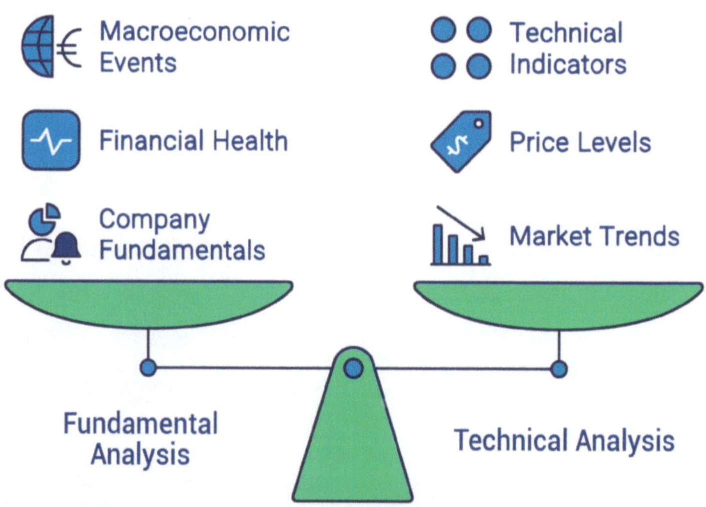

Balancing Fundamental and Technical Analysis in Stock Trading

Gut Feeling and Market Sentiment

- Evaluate Market Sentiment: Hopeful or Fearful?
- Adapt to Market Strategies: Momentum, Value, etc.
- Float like a Jellyfish: Let the Market Push You

Position Sizing and Risk Management

- Test Positions to Get a Feel for the Market
- Trade Smaller During Uncertain Periods
- Play Defense: Downsize Positions if Needed
- Never Risk Too Much on One Event or Company
- Force Yourself to Trade Against the Consensus

Trading Rules and Discipline

- Be Patient—Wait for the Opportunity
- Trade on Your Own Ideas and Style
- Never Trade Impulsively, Especially on Others' Advice
- Listen to the Market, Not Outside Opinions
- Anticipate, Don't React
- Think Trades Through Before You Put Them On
- If Unsure About a Position, Just Get Out
- Be Flexible and Admit When You Are Wrong
- Recognize Winners and Losers Fast

Become a Successful Trader

Psychological Mindset

- Remain Confident—Opportunities Never Stop
- Start Each Day from Last Night's Close, Not Your Original Cost
- Get Rid of All Distractions
- Be Totally Flexible and Open to Changing Your Mind

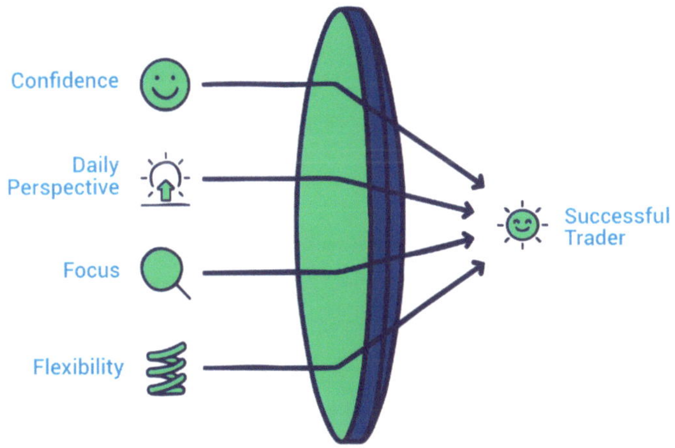

Review and Learn from Mistakes

- Acknowledge Mistakes and Learn from Them
- Develop a Six-Month and One-Year Outlook
- Recognize Market's Reaction to Data as a Warning Flag
- Force Yourself to Buy on Extreme Weakness and Sell on Extreme Strength

By adhering to this comprehensive framework, traders can navigate the complexities of the market with confidence and skill, ultimately leading to more successful trading outcomes.

Notes

Notes

Notes

Notes

Notes

Notes

Monthly Review

Schedule a regular review of the investments to assess performance against expectations.

Month	
Assessment	

02

MACRO VIEW ASSESS MARKET

Market Analysis and Strategic Action Plan

This section outlines a framework for assessing market conditions, evaluating liquidity, analyzing inflation trends, and monitoring market movements. It provides a structured approach to understanding the current economic landscape and offers actionable items to adapt investment strategies accordingly. The flowchart illustrates the interconnectedness of various market indicators and the necessary steps to take in response to changing conditions.

1 Assess Market Conditions

Start: Assess Market Conditions

- Review growth momentum and liquidity conditions.
- Analyze inflation trends and monitor market movements.
- Evaluate the outlook for Bitcoin and cryptocurrencies.

Factors Contributing to Market Condition Assessment

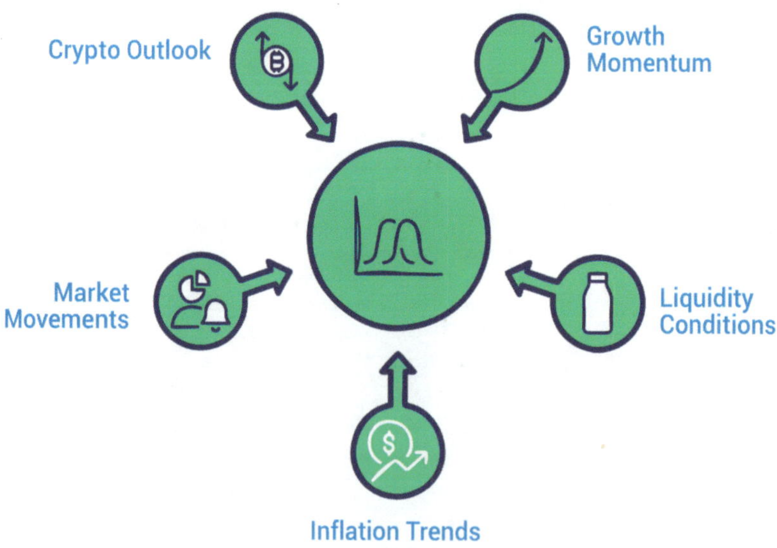

1.1 Review Growth Momentum

- ISM Index Analysis
- NFIB Small Business Optimism Index

How to best assess growth momentum?

ISM Index Analysis

Leading indicator of manufacturing activity, providing insights into short-term economic trends.

NFIB Small Business Optimism Index

Gauge of small business confidence and sentiment, reflecting their outlook on the economy

1.2 Evaluate Liquidity Conditions

- Financial Conditions Index
- PBOC Liquidity Injection
- Total Liquidity Index Breakout

Evaluation Liquidity Conditions in China

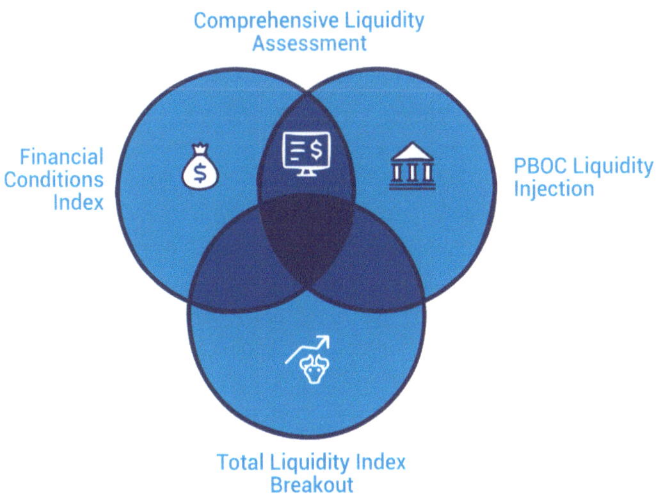

1.3 Analyze Inflation Trends

- Review CPI Data
- Core CPI Projection
- NFIB Price Raising Plans

Key Indicators of Inflation Trends

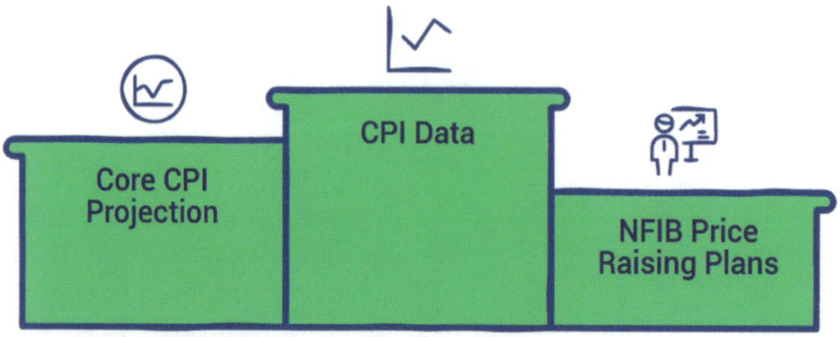

1.4 Monitor Market Movements

- Nasdaq Corrections
- Sector Performance Analysis
- Dollar Weakening Impact

Key Factors Influencing Market Conditions

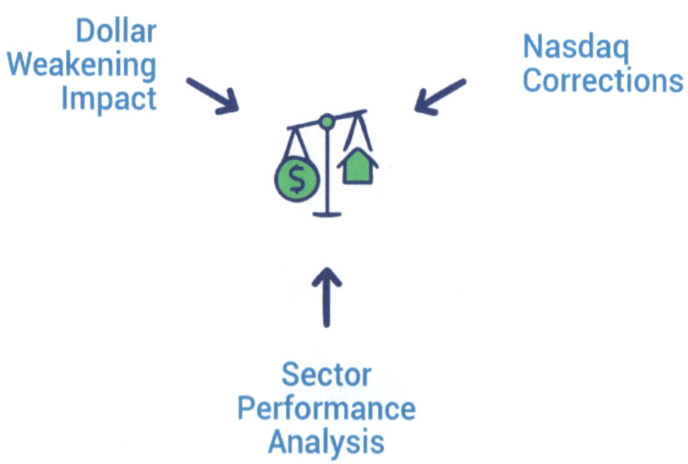

1.5 Bitcoin & Cryptocurrencies Outlook

- Liquidity Impact on Bitcoin
- Bitcoin Volatility Analysis

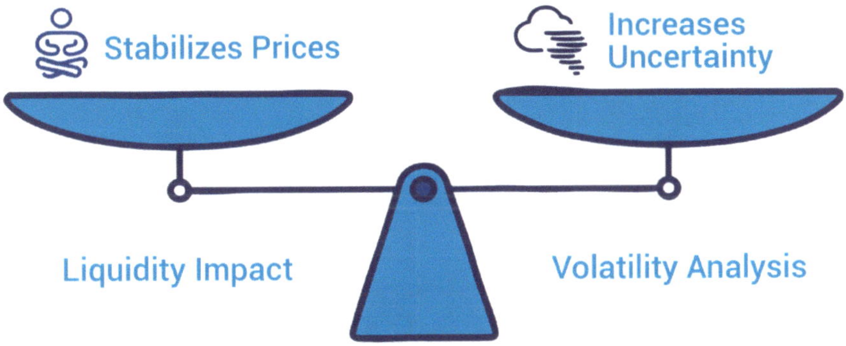

Balancing liquidity and volatility in Bitcoin

1.6 Assess Unemployment Data

The first step in this process is to assess the unemployment data available from various sources, such as government reports, labor statistics, and economic research institutions. This assessment involves gathering the most recent and relevant data to ensure an accurate analysis.

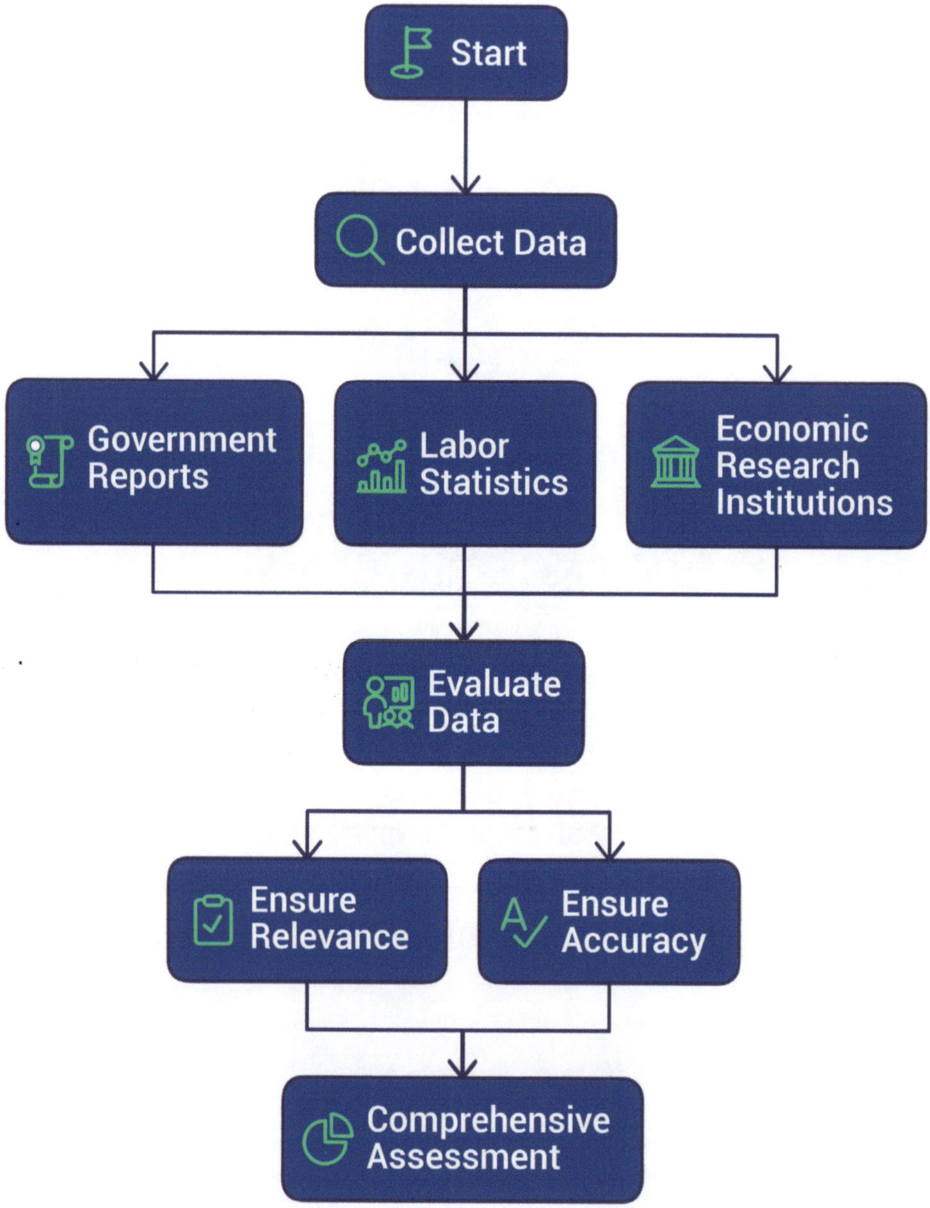
Start
Collect Data
Government Reports
Labor Statistics
Economic Research Institutions
Evaluate Data
Ensure Relevance
Ensure Accuracy
Comprehensive Assessment

1.7 Review Unemployment Rate Trends

Once the unemployment data has been collected, the next step is to review the trends in the unemployment rate over time. This involves analyzing historical data to identify patterns, fluctuations, and potential correlations with economic events or policies. By understanding these trends, stakeholders can make informed decisions and predictions regarding future labor market conditions.

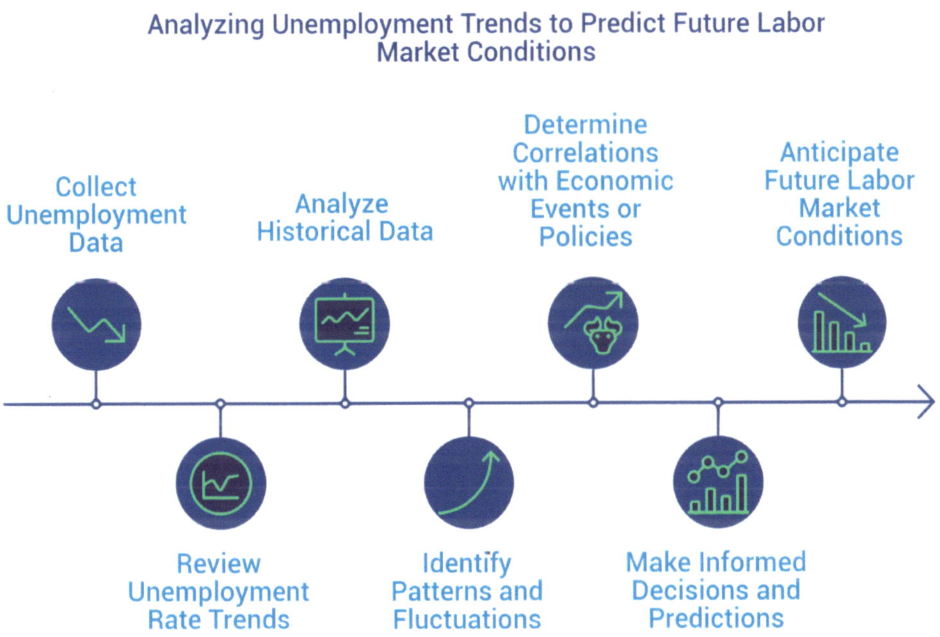

2 Actionable Items

- Monitor Liquidity Conditions
- Align Investment Strategies
- Watch for Market Corrections
- Prepare for Bitcoin Price Increases

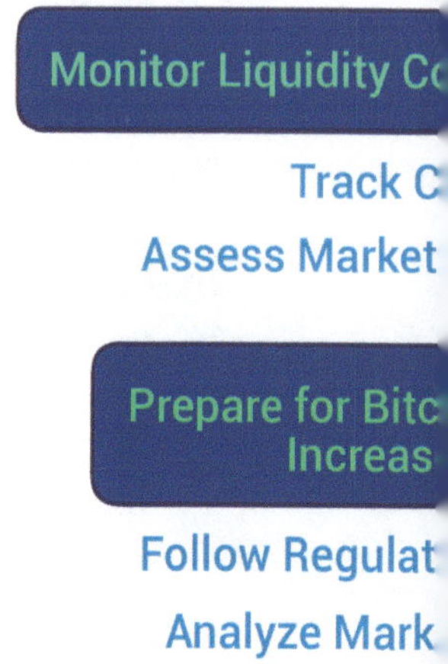

3 Conclusion

Stay Vigilant & Adapt Strategies

This structured approach ensures that investors remain informed and prepared to navigate the complexities of the market, allowing for timely adjustments to investment strategies based on evolving economic indicators.

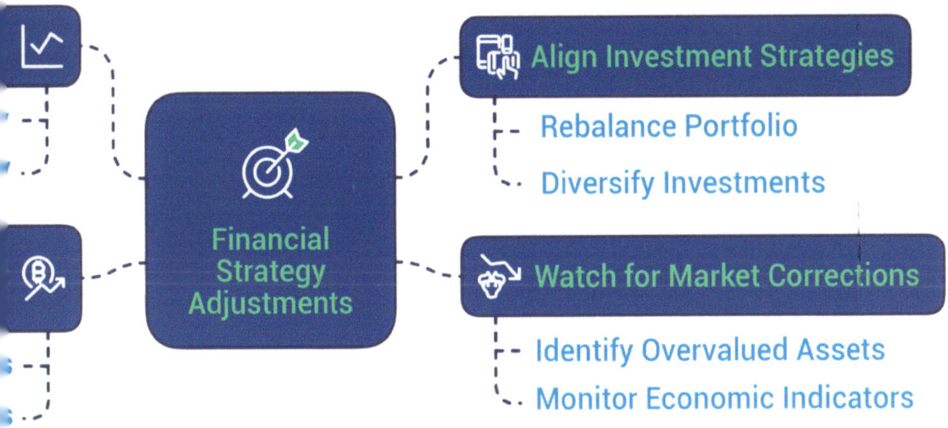
Financial Strategy Adjustments
Align Investment Strategies
Rebalance Portfolio
Diversify Investments
Watch for Market Corrections
Identify Overvalued Assets
Monitor Economic Indicators

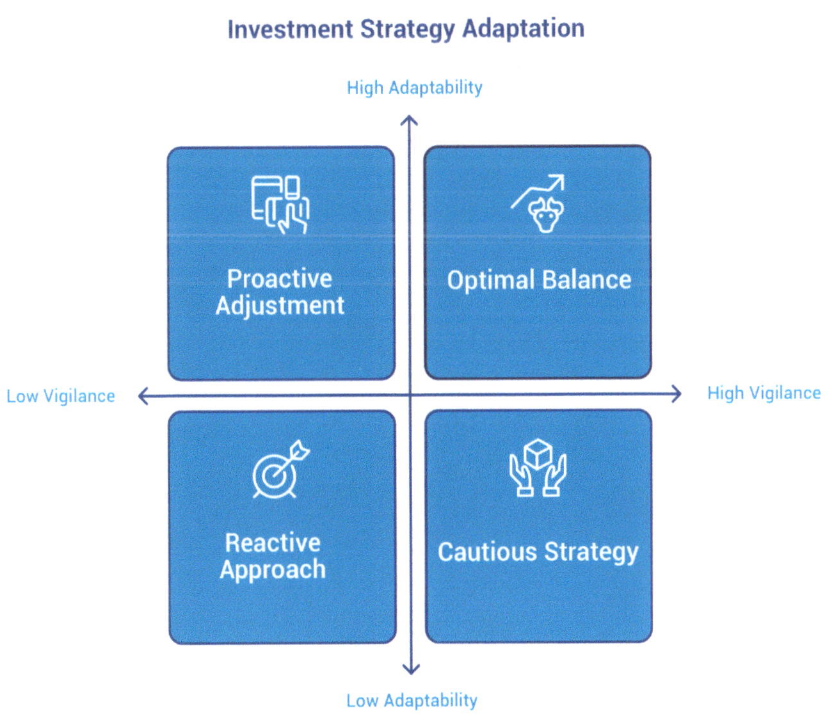
Investment Strategy Adaptation
High Adaptability
Proactive Adjustment
Optimal Balance
Low Vigilance
High Vigilance
Reactive Approach
Cautious Strategy
Low Adaptability

Notes

Notes

Notes

Notes

Notes

Notes

Monthly Review

Schedule a regular review of the investments to assess performance against expectations.

Month	
Assessment	

03

TRADING LESSONS

Ultimate Trading Worksheet

This section outlines a comprehensive trading strategy through a structured worksheet that guides traders from the foundational concepts of wealth and optionality to advanced trading techniques. Each step is designed to build upon the previous one, ensuring a holistic approach to trading that emphasizes adaptability, critical thinking, and a keen awareness of market dynamics.

Step 1 Wealth = Optionality

Understanding that wealth is fundamentally about having options is crucial. This step emphasizes the importance of creating opportunities for yourself in trading.

Wealth and Optionality

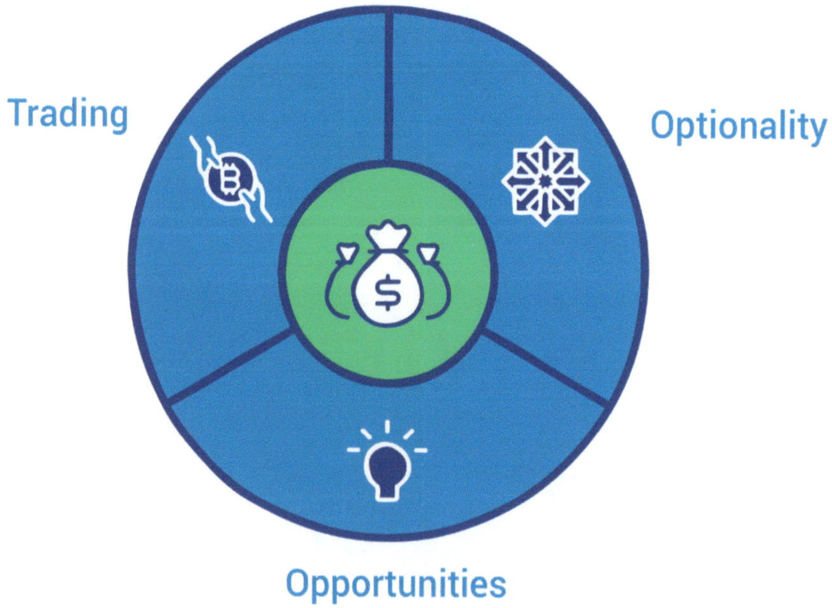

Step 2 Find Something That Interests You

Identify a market or asset class that captivates your interest. Passion can drive more in-depth research and better decision-making.

Passion-Driven Investment Process

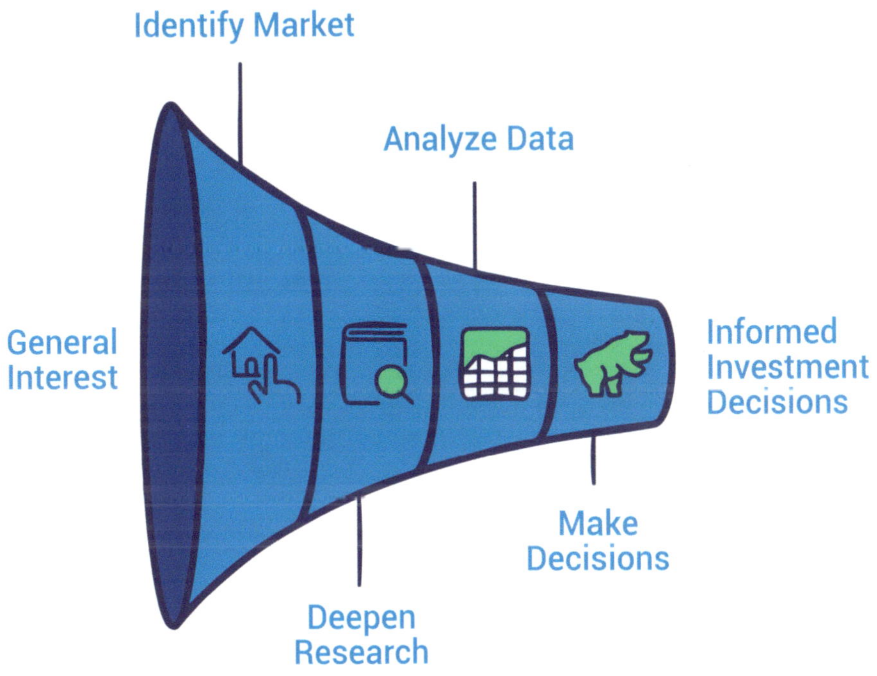

Step 3 Don't Underestimate the Value of Luck and Timing

Recognize that luck and timing play significant roles in trading success. While skill is essential, being in the right place at the right time can make a substantial difference.

Step 4 The Power of Trade Construction

Learn how to construct trades effectively. This involves understanding the mechanics of trades and how to optimize them for better outcomes.

Trade Construction Hierarchy

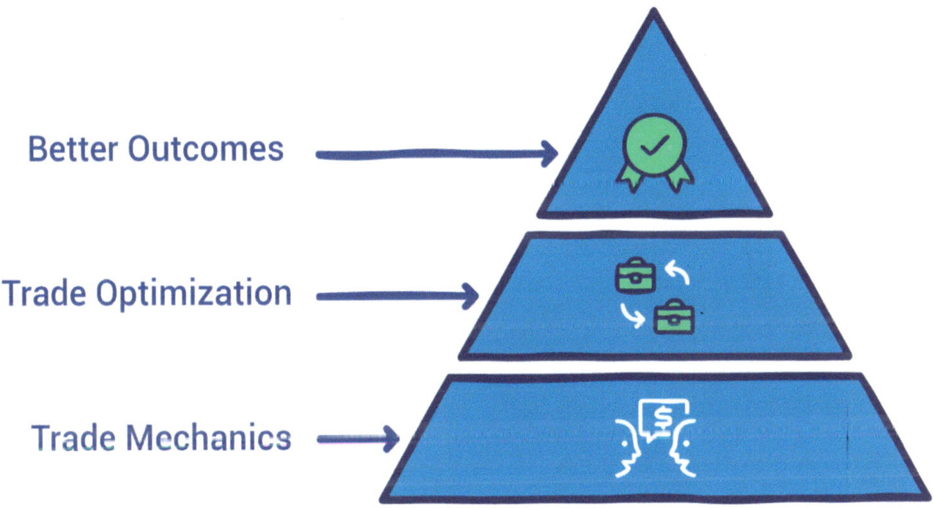

Step 5 Directional Trading Can Pay Off

Directional trading, or betting on the movement of an asset, can yield significant returns. This step encourages traders to develop a directional bias based on their analysis.

Maximize Returns through Directional Trading

Step 6 Big Opportunities Come from Questioning Wrong Assumptions

Challenge your assumptions about the market. This critical thinking can uncover opportunities that others may overlook.

Cycle of Uncovering Market Opportunities

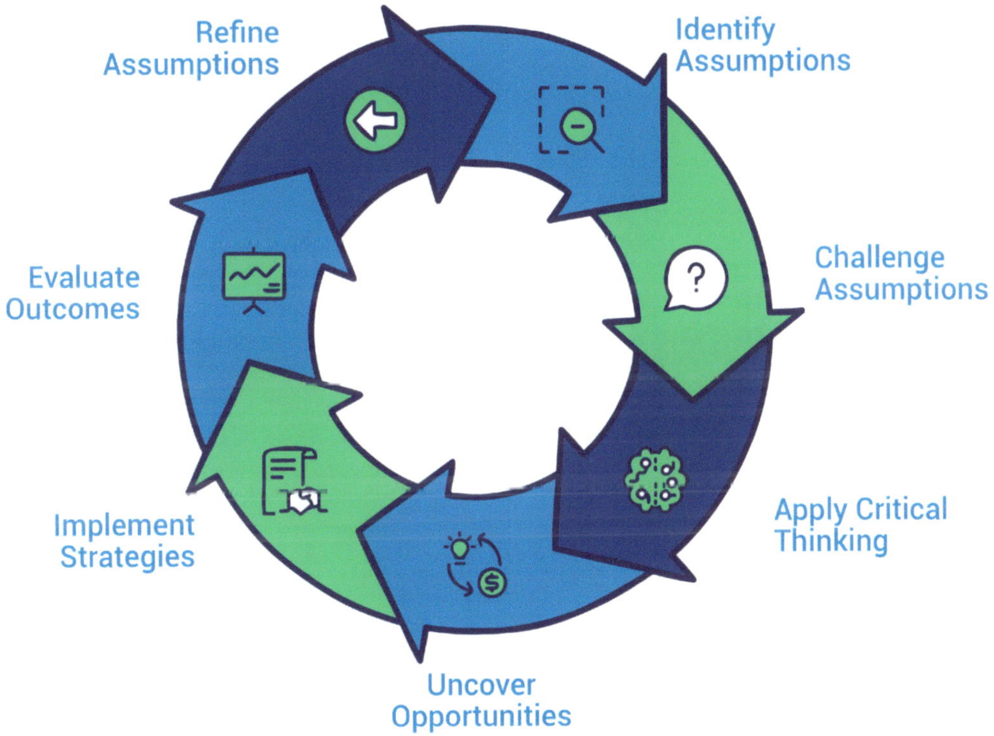

Step 7 If You're Struggling, Go Back to Basics

When facing difficulties, revisiting fundamental concepts can provide clarity and help refocus your trading strategy.

Revisiting Fundamentals in Trading

Pros	VS	Cons
Clarity		Time-consuming
Refocus strategy		Potential frustration
Build confidence		Risk of over-analysis
Identify mistakes		May feel repetitive
Strengthen foundation		Short-term setback

Step 8 Pay Attention to the Facts not the Noise

In a world filled with information, it's vital to distinguish between useful data and distractions. Focus on facts that influence your trading decisions.

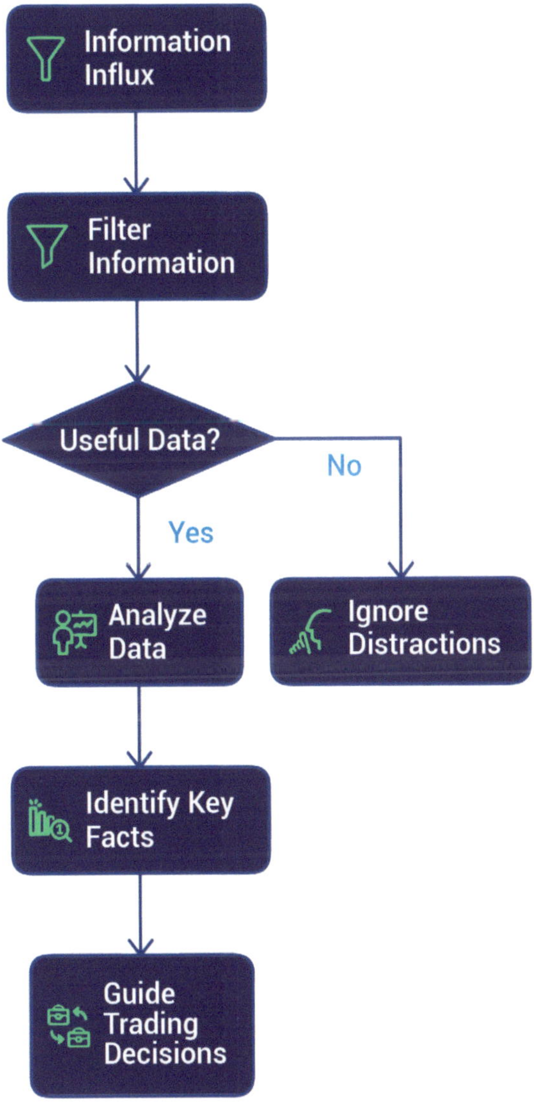

Step 9 Adapt Position Size According to the Market Regime

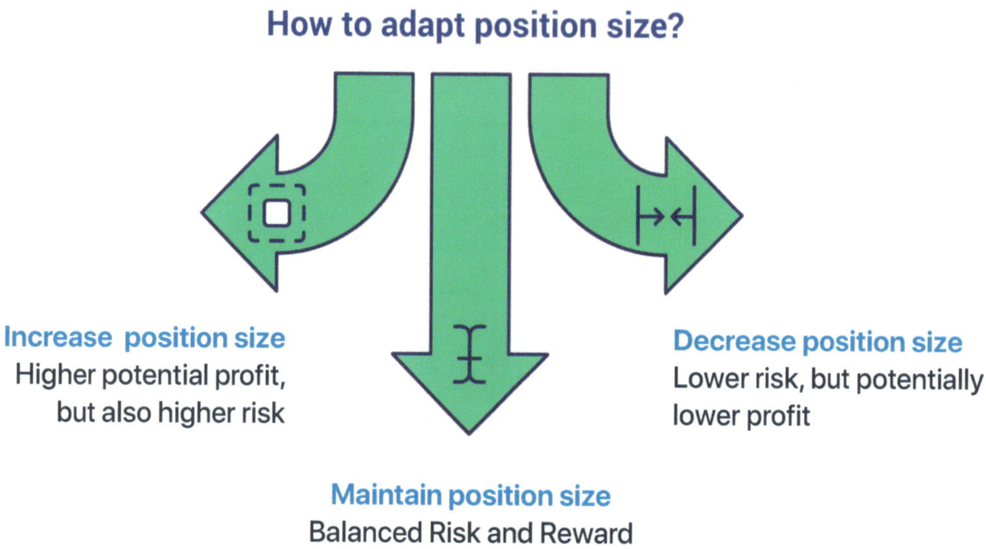

Adjust your position sizes based on the current market conditions. This flexibility can help manage risk and enhance profitability.

Step 10 Figure Out Your Edge

Identify what sets you apart as a trader. Understanding your unique advantages can lead to more informed and confident trading decisions.

Identifying Unique Trading Advantages

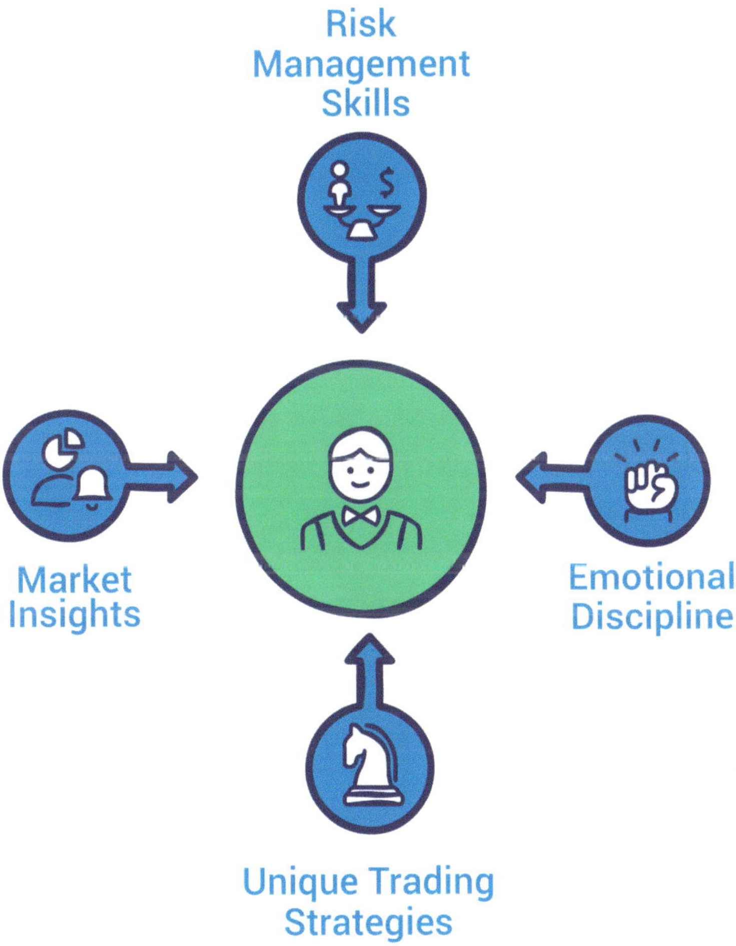

Step 11 The Best Investors Adapt to Change

The most successful investors are those who can pivot and adapt to changing market conditions. Embrace change as a constant in the trading landscape.

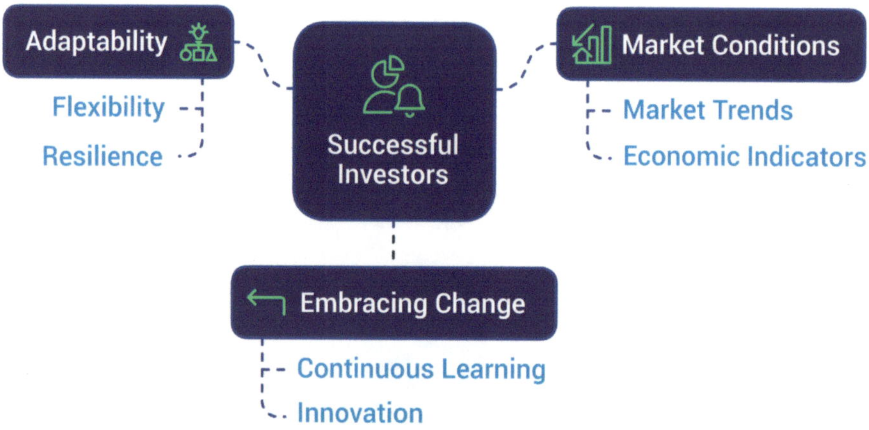

By following this structured approach, traders can enhance their skills and improve their chances of success in the dynamic world of trading.

Trade Smart, Succeed Boldly!

Notes

Notes

Notes

Notes

Notes

Notes

Notes

Notes

Monthly Review

Schedule a regular review of the investments to assess performance against expectations.

Month	
Assessment	

Quarterly Review

Schedule a regular review of the investments to assess performance against expectations.

Quarter	
Assessment	

04

ESSENTIAL STEPS FOR SUCCESSFUL TRADING

This section presents a structured flowchart designed to guide traders through essential steps for successful trading. It emphasizes the importance of mindset, risk management, position sizing, emotional stability, and analysis techniques. Each step is broken down into actionable components, providing a comprehensive approach to trading that can help traders achieve their financial goals.

Step 1 Mindset and Belief

Believe it's possible to make it successful

Cultivating a positive mindset is crucial for success in trading.

Key to Trading Success

Step 2 Risk Management

Focus on not losing money

Prioritize protecting your capital.

Manage emotional tolerance

Understand your emotional limits to avoid impulsive decisions.

Step 3 Position Sizing

Risk 1-2% of capital per trade

This helps in managing losses effectively.

Trade small, reduce position size

Start with smaller trades to minimize risk.

How to manage position size?

Risk 1-2% of capital per trade

Helps in managing losses effectively

Trade small, reduce position size

Minimize risk by starting with smaller trades

Step 3 Emotional Equilibrium

Maintain emotional equilibrium

Stay calm and composed while trading.

Stop trading if equilibrium is disturbed

Recognize when to take a break to avoid emotional trading.

Balance emotional control in trading

Step 5 Fundamental and Technical Analysis

Develop a fundamental market view

Understand the broader market context.

Use technical analysis to confirm the view

Analyze price movements and patterns.

Trade when fundamental and technical analysis align

Look for confluence between both analyses for better trading opportunities.

Trading Strategy Refinement

This flowchart serves as a roadmap for traders, ensuring they cover all critical aspects of trading to enhance their chances of success.

Notes

Notes

Notes

Notes

Notes

Notes

Notes

Monthly Review

Schedule a regular review of the investments to assess performance against expectations.

Month	
Assessment	

05

TRADERS' SKILLS AND MINDSET

This section outlines a comprehensive trading worksheet designed to enhance traders' skills and mindset. It covers essential aspects such as vision, risk management, trader psychology, macroeconomic factors, price action mastery, and the Heisenberg principle in trading. Each section provides insights and actionable strategies to improve trading performance and decision-making.

Having the Necessary Vision

Imagine Alternative Scenarios

Envision different market outcomes to prepare for various possibilities.

Consensus not Confirmed by the Market

Be cautious of widely held beliefs that lack market validation.

Form Mental Pictures of the World

Create mental models to visualize market dynamics and potential movements.

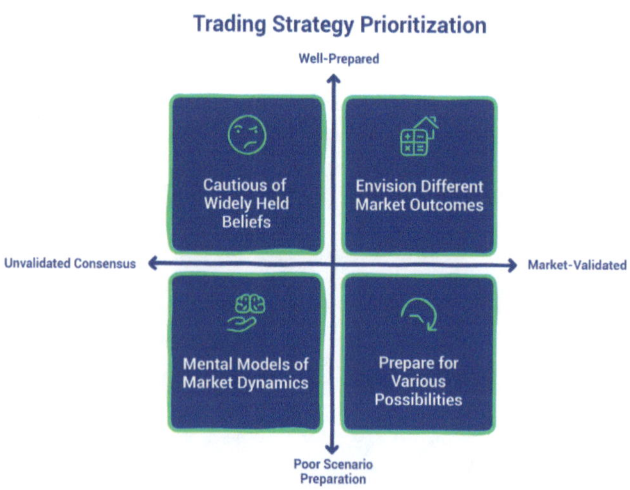

Importance of Risk Management

Don't Lose Money for Unknown Reasons

Identify and mitigate risks to protect your capital.

Undertrade and Manage Position Size

Focus on quality over quantity in your trades.

Predetermined Stop-Loss

Set stop-loss levels before entering trades to limit potential losses.

Avoid Highly Correlated Positions

Diversify your portfolio to reduce risk exposure

Risk Management Strategies

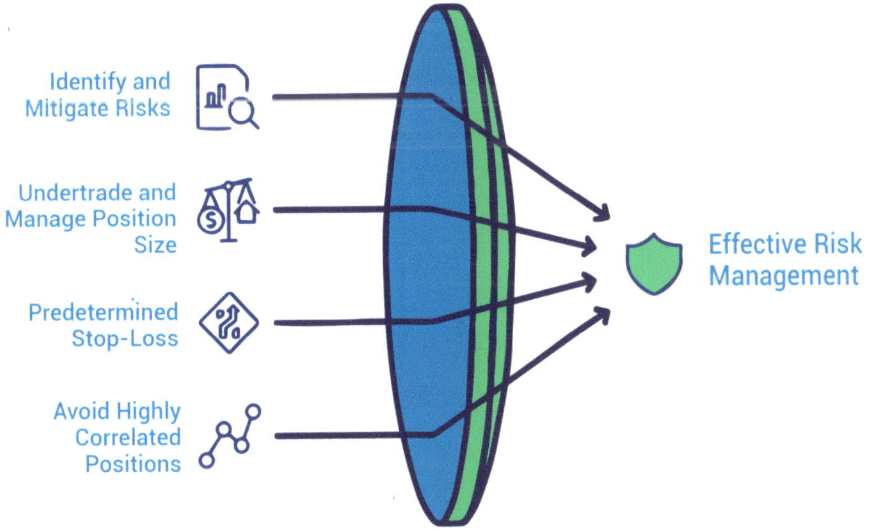

Trader's Mindset

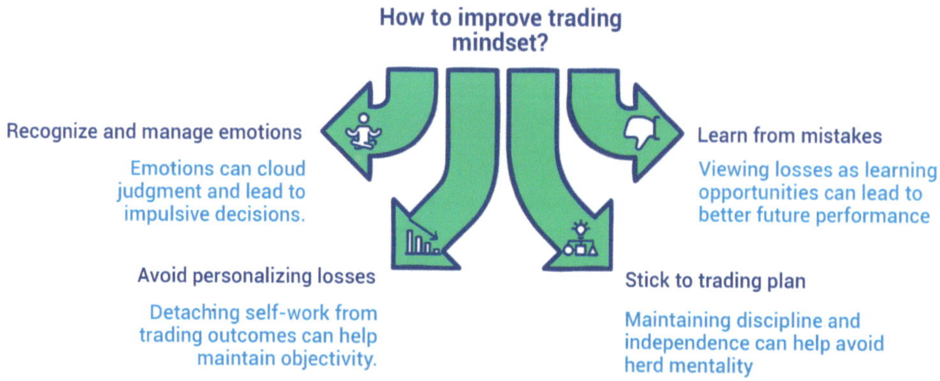

Close Positions if Emotionally Disturbed

Recognize when emotions cloud judgment and act accordingly.

Accept Mistakes and Learn

View losses as learning opportunities to improve future performance.

Avoid Personalizing Losses

Detach your self-worth from trading outcomes to maintain objectivity.

Maintain Discipline and Independence

Stick to your trading plan and avoid herd mentality.

Importance of Macro

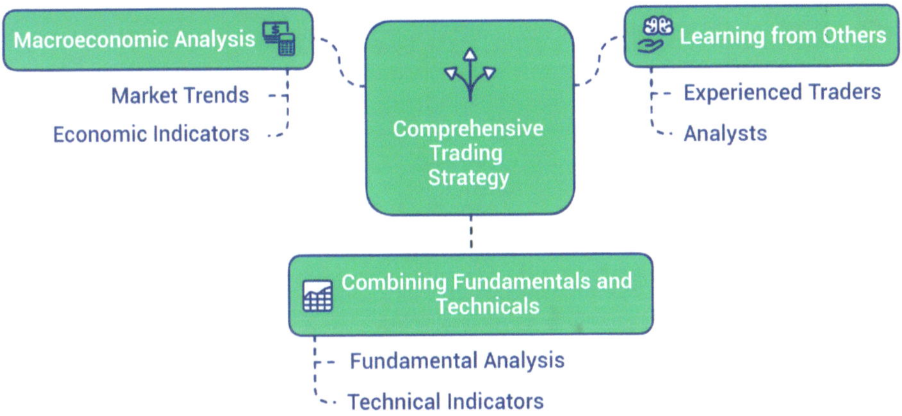

Trade on Market View, Not Just Technicals

Incorporate macroeconomic analysis into your trading strategy.

Leverage Knowledge from Others

Learn from experienced traders and analysts to enhance your understanding.

Use Fundamentals Alongside Technicals

Combine fundamental analysis with technical indicators for a well-rounded approach.

Mastering Price Action

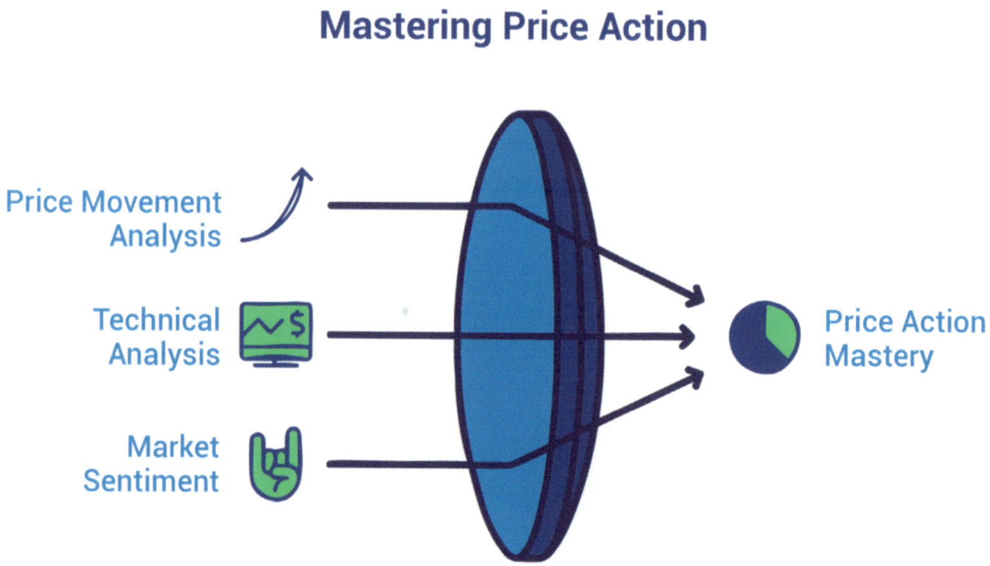

Study Price Movements and Patterns

Analyze historical price data to identify trends and reversals.

Use Technical Analysis as a Tool, Not a Predictor

Utilize technical indicators to inform decisions, not dictate them.

Identify Disequilibria and Market Sentiment

Recognize imbalances in supply and demand to capitalize on trading opportunities.

The Heisenberg Principle in Trading

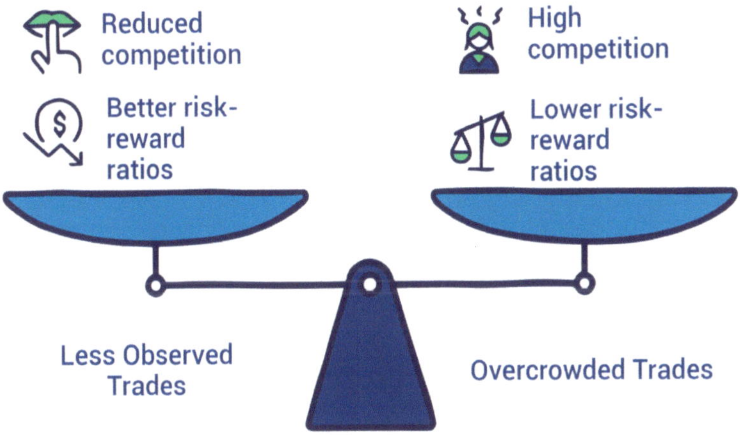

Choose less observed trades for better risk-reward ratios and reduced competition.

Less Observed Trades are Better

Focus on less popular trades that may offer better risk-reward ratios.

Avoid Overcrowded Trades

Steer clear of trades that are heavily populated by other traders to reduce competition.

Look for Breakouts with Minimal Speculation

Seek out breakout opportunities that are supported by solid fundamentals rather than mere speculation

This worksheet serves as a guide for traders to refine their strategies and enhance their trading acumen. By focusing on these key areas, traders can improve their decision-making processes and ultimately achieve better trading results.

Notes

Notes

Notes

Notes

Notes

Notes

Monthly Review

Schedule a regular review of the investments to assess performance against expectations.

Month	
Assessment	

06

IMPORTANCE OF GOAL SETTING

This section outlines a comprehensive flowchart for an "Ultimate Trading Worksheet," designed to guide traders through a structured approach to trading. The flowchart emphasizes the importance of setting goals, applying discipline, and continuously learning from market behaviors. Each step is interconnected, providing a clear pathway from goal setting to trade execution and evaluation.

Steps

Step 1 Set a Goal

Establish clear and achievable trading objectives.

How to start trading?

Set a Goal

Clear and achievable trading objectives

No Goal

Trade aimless without a clear objective

Step 2 Apply Discipline and Consistency

Maintain a disciplined approach to trading, ensuring consistency in actions.

Cycle of Discipline and Consistency in Trading

Step 3 Imagine Alternative Scenarios

Consider various market scenarios and their potential impacts on trades.

How to approach market scenarios?

Reactive VS **Proactive**

Reactive

Analyze scenarios as they unfold

Proactive

Anticipate scenarios and prepare for them

Step 4 Wait for Market Confirmation

Look for confirmation signals in the market before proceeding with trades.

Step 5 Identify the Consensus That the Market Is Not Confirming

Analyze market sentiment and identify discrepancies between consensus and market behavior.

Market Sentiment Analysis Cycle

Step 6 Position Sizing and Risk Management

Determine appropriate position sizes and implement risk management strategies.

Components of Position Sizing and Risk Management

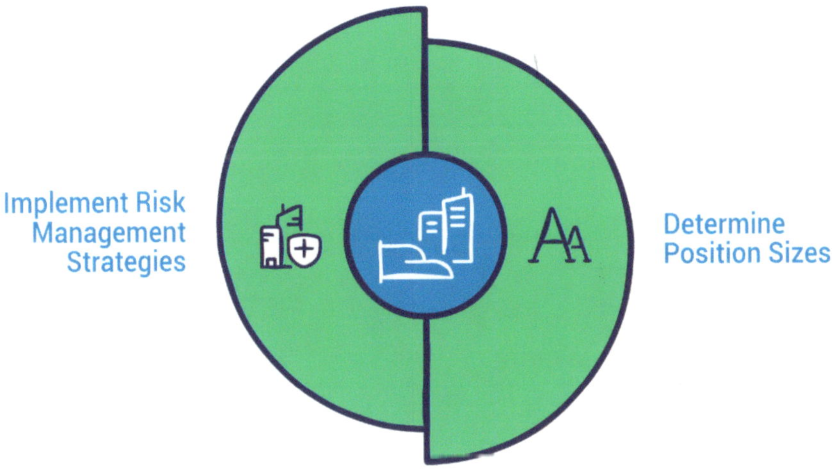

Step 7 Set Predetermined Stop Levels

Establish stop-loss levels to protect against significant losses.

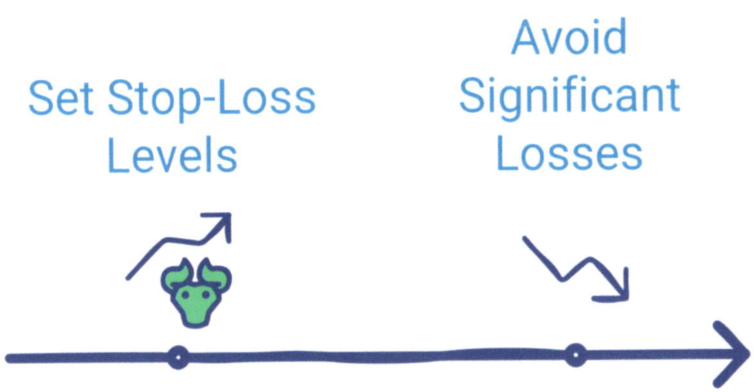

Step 8 Analyze Technical and Fundamental Data

Conduct thorough analysis of both technical indicators and fundamental factors affecting the market.

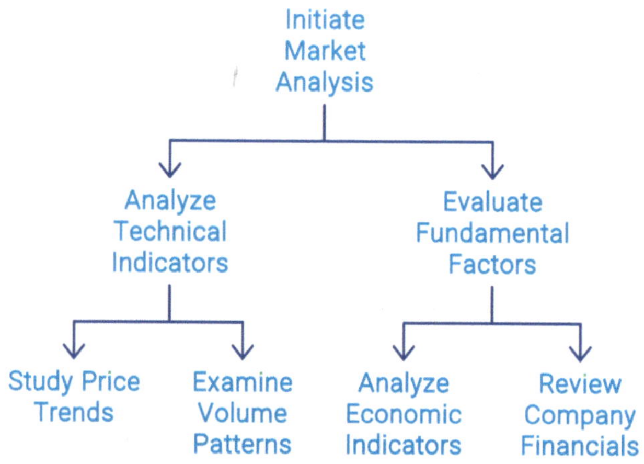

Step 9 Observe and Interpret Market Behavior

Monitor market movements and interpret behaviors to inform trading decisions.

Observing and Interpreting Market Behavior

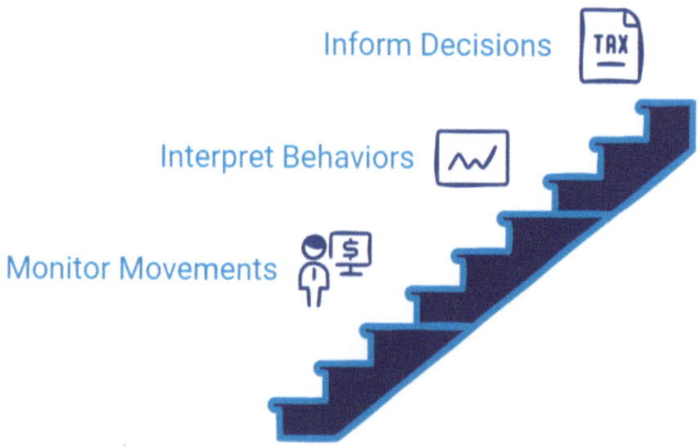

Step 10 Execute the Trade

Carry out the trade based on the analysis and strategy.

Trading Execution Cycle

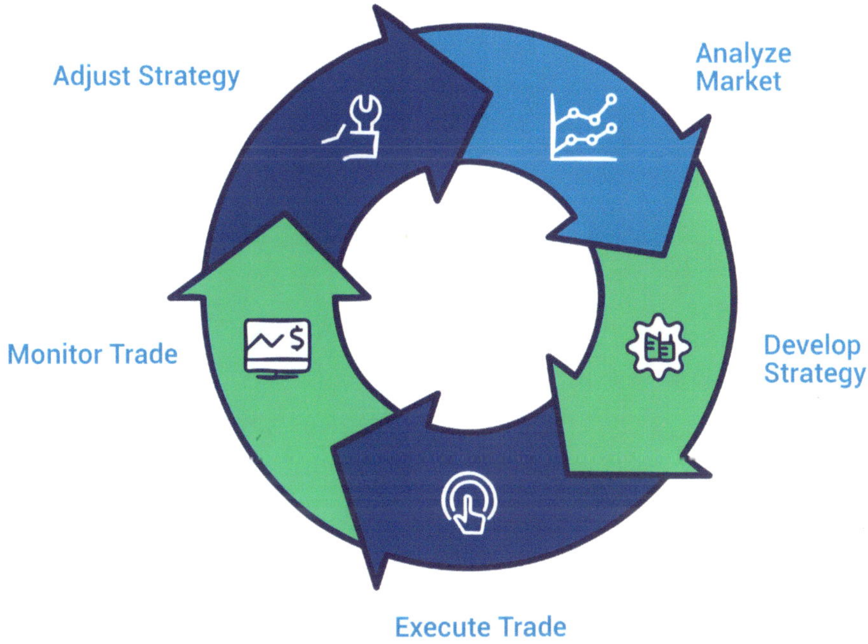

Step 11 Review and Adjust Position

Regularly review the position and make adjustments as necessary.

Step 12 Continuous Learning and Improvement

Engage in ongoing education to improve trading skills and strategies.

Continuous Learning in Trading

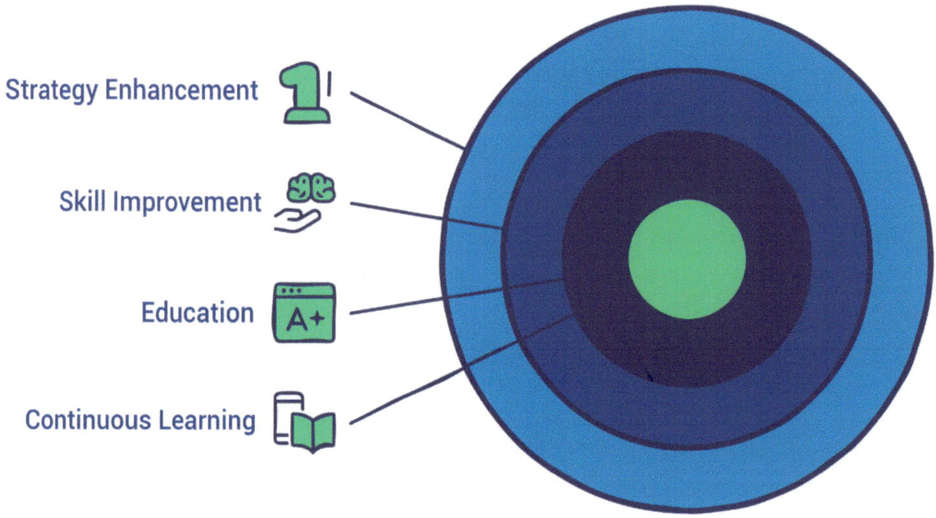

Additional Considerations

Reduce Position Size if Necessary

If market conditions change, consider reducing position sizes to mitigate risk.

Establish a Stop Based on Technical Levels

Set stops based on technical analysis to enhance risk management.

Assess Correlation Between Positions

Evaluate the correlation between different positions to avoid overexposure.

Minimize Position Size Based on Risk Tolerance

Adjust position sizes according to individual risk tolerance levels.

Trade Monitoring

Monitor Trade and Adhere to Stops

Keep a close watch on trades and adhere to stop-loss levels.

Exit Trade if Stop is Triggered

Be prepared to exit trades if stop-loss levels are hit.

Evaluate Trade Outcome

After exiting, assess the outcome of the trade for future learning.

Market Analysis

Look for Unusual Market Behavior

Stay alert for any unusual market movements that could indicate opportunities or risks.

Formulate Trading Hypotheses

Develop hypotheses based on observed market behaviors.

Refine Strategies Based on Analysis

Continuously refine trading strategies based on ongoing analysis and market feedback.

Market Analysis and Strategy Refinement

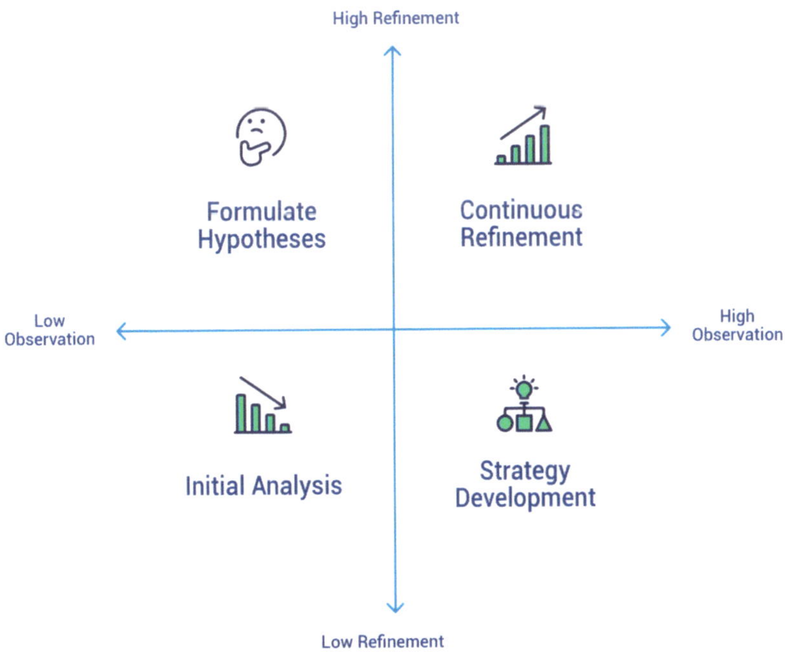

Documentation and Learning

Document Lessons Learned

Keep a record of lessons learned from each trade to enhance future performance.

Apply Lessons to Future Trades

Use documented lessons to inform and improve future trading decisions.

This flowchart serves as a valuable tool for traders seeking to enhance their trading practices through structured analysis and disciplined execution.

Notes

Notes

Notes

Notes

Notes

Notes

Notes

Notes

Monthly Review

Schedule a regular review of the investments to assess performance against expectations.

Month	
Assessment	

Quarterly Review

Schedule a regular review of the investments to assess performance against expectations.

Quarter	
Assessment	

07 IDENTIFYING MARKET OPPORTUNITIES

This section outlines a strategic framework for identifying rare market opportunities and effectively capitalizing on them. It emphasizes the importance of market analysis, risk management, and emotional discipline in trading. Each step in the process is interconnected, creating a comprehensive approach to navigating market conditions and maximizing potential gains.

Steps

Step 1 Identify Rare Opportunities

Begin by scanning the market for unique investment opportunities that stand out due to their potential for high returns.

Where to invest?

Rare Opportunities
High potential returns

VS

Common Opportunities
Lower potential returns

Step 2 Analyze Market Conditions

Conduct a thorough analysis of current market conditions to understand trends, volatility, and other factors that may impact investment decisions.

Market Conditions and Investment Decisions

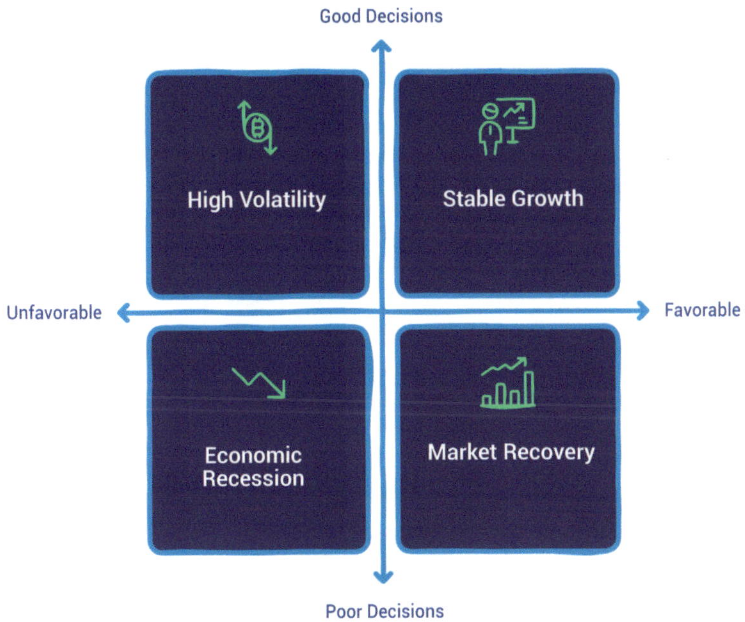

Step 3 Understand Government Policies and Market Reactions

Stay informed about relevant government policies and how they influence market behavior. This understanding can provide insights into potential market movements.

Influence of Government Policies on Market Reactions

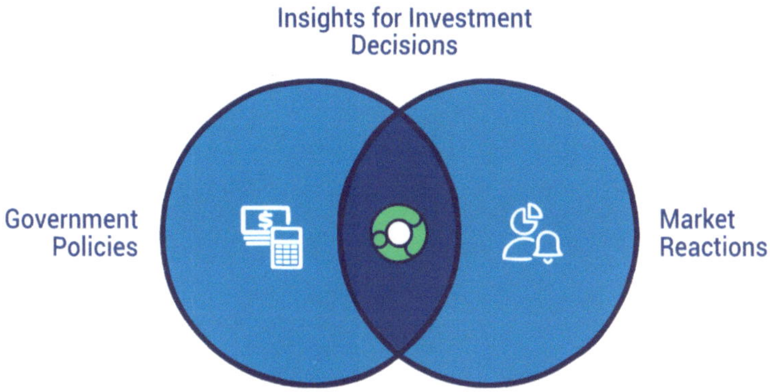

Step 4 Take Advantage of Clear Market Signals

Look for clear signals in the market that indicate a favorable time to enter a position. This could include technical indicators or significant news events.

Identifying Favorable Market Entry

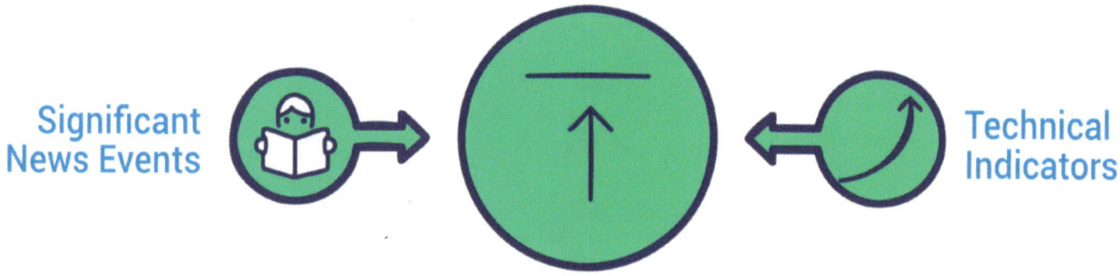

Step 5 Position Sizing Based on Conviction

Determine the size of your position based on your level of conviction in the opportunity. A higher conviction may warrant a larger position size.

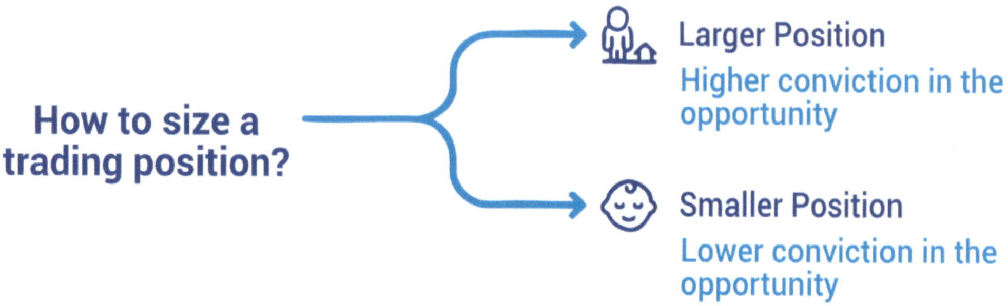

Step 6 Risk Control: Immediate Exit on Losses

Implement strict risk control measures. If a position moves against you, be prepared to exit immediately to minimize losses.

Step 7 Evaluate and Adjust Position Size

Continuously evaluate your positions and adjust the size as necessary based on market conditions and your ongoing analysis.

Step 8 Monitor Emotional State and Market Conditions

Keep track of your emotional state while trading. Emotional decisions can lead to poor outcomes, so maintaining objectivity is crucial.

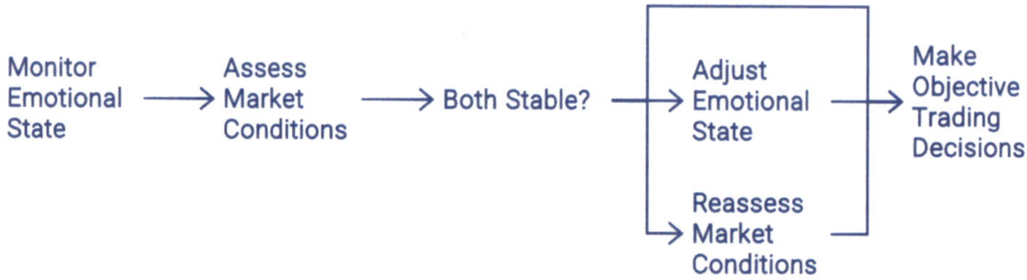

Step 9 Gradually Increase Position When Winning

If a position is performing well, consider gradually increasing your position size to capitalize on the momentum

Capitalize on Winning Positions

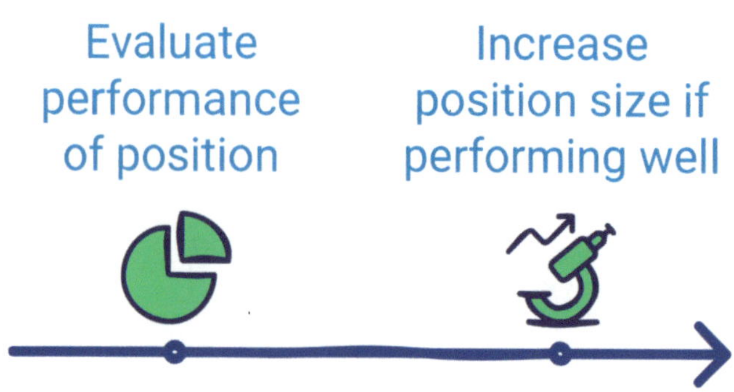

Step 10 Stay Disciplined and Objective

Throughout the process, maintain discipline and objectivity. Avoid letting emotions dictate your trading decisions to ensure consistent performance.

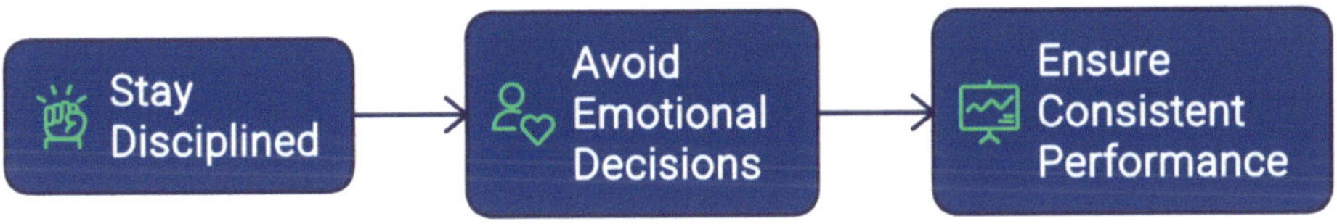

By following this strategic framework, traders can enhance their ability to identify and act on rare market opportunities while managing risk effectively.

Notes

Notes

Notes

Notes

Notes

Notes

Monthly Review

Schedule a regular review of the investments to assess performance against expectations.

Month	
Assessment	

08 TRADING FRAMEWORK

This section outlines a comprehensive framework for traders to enhance their trading strategies through a structured approach. It emphasizes the importance of identifying one's edge, understanding market behavior, implementing risk management, and setting exit strategies. The worksheet serves as a guide to navigate the complexities of trading while maintaining discipline and rationality.

Trading Framework

Identify your Edge

Understanding what sets you apart as a trader is crucial. This involves recognizing your strengths and weaknesses, as well as the unique strategies that work best for you.

What sets you apart as a trader?

Strengths

Leverage your expertise and experience

Weaknesses

Address and mitigate your limitations

Analyze Market Behavior

Study the market trends and behaviors to make informed decisions. This includes understanding price movements, volume changes, and other indicators that can impact your trades.

Implement Risk Management

Risk management is essential to protect your capital. This involves setting rules and guidelines to minimize losses and manage your overall exposure in the market.

Monitor Market Volatility

Stay aware of market volatility, as it can significantly affect your trading outcomes. Being prepared for sudden changes can help you make timely decisions.

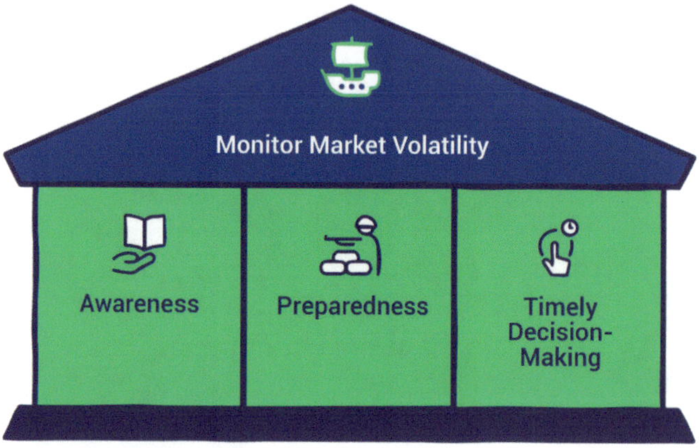

Set Exit Strategies

Having clear exit strategies is vital for successful trading. This includes knowing when to take profits and when to cut losses to maintain a healthy trading portfolio.

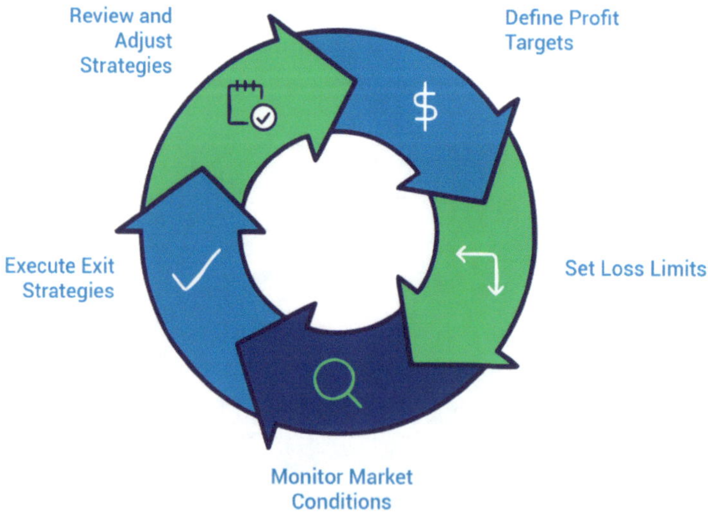

Understand Probabilities

Grasping the concept of probabilities can enhance your decision-making process. This involves assessing the likelihood of various market scenarios and outcomes.

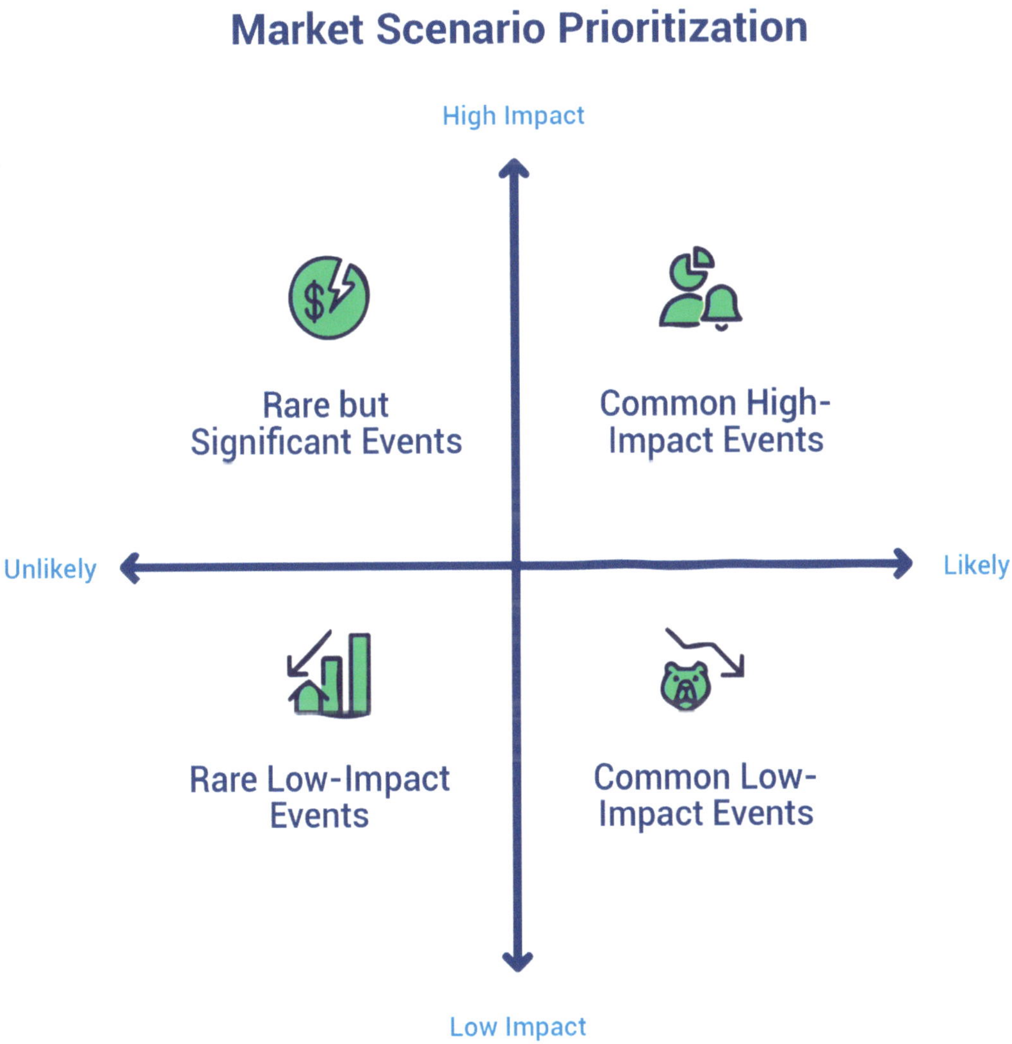

Recognize Non-Normal Distributions

Markets often do not follow a normal distribution. Understanding this can help you better prepare for unexpected market movements.

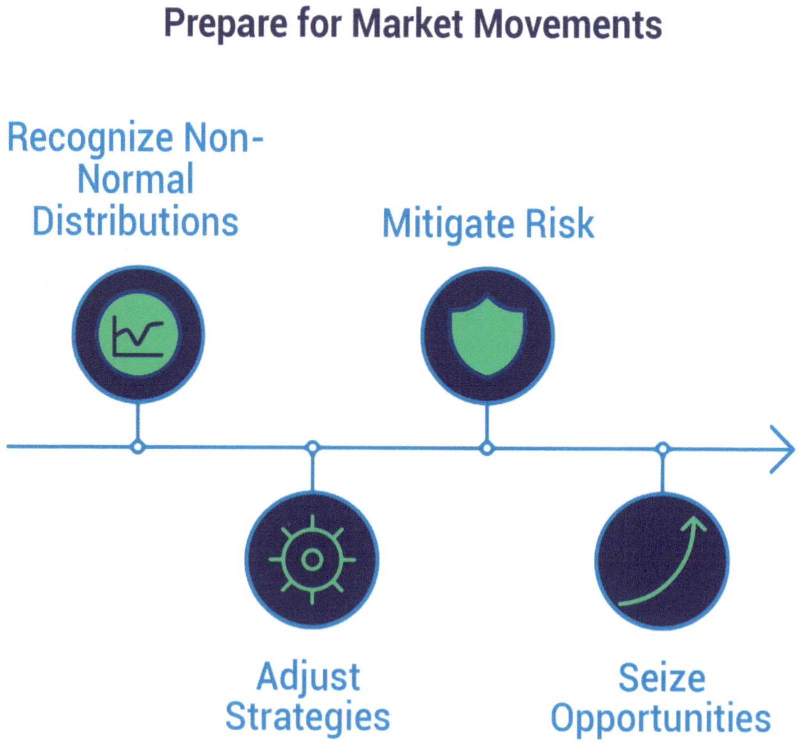

Apply Risk Control Rules

Implement specific rules to manage risk effectively:

- **Rule 1:** Exit if Loss > X% Equity
- **Rule 2:** Liquidate if Down X% in a Day
- **Rule 3:** Stop Trading if Monthly Loss > X%
- **Rule 4:** Limit Position Size Monthly

Risk Management Funnel

Execute Planned Exits

Stick to your exit strategies to ensure you remain disciplined in your trading approach.

Discipline in Trading

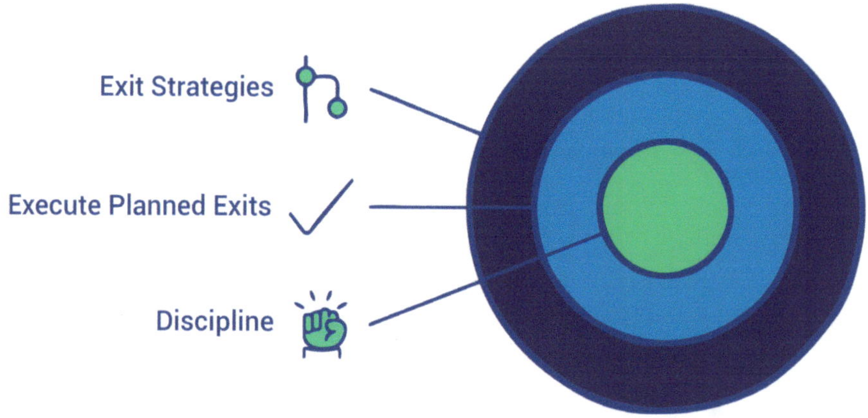

Stay Rational & Remove Bias

Maintaining a rational mindset is crucial. Avoid emotional decisions that can lead to impulsive trading actions.

How to approach trading?

Rational

Avoid impulsive decisions

Emotional

May lead to impulsive actions

Avoid Emotional Decisions

Emotions can cloud judgment. Focus on your trading plan and avoid letting feelings dictate your actions.

Components of Effective Trading Decision-Making

Ensure Longevity in the Market

By following these guidelines, you can work towards ensuring your longevity and success in the trading market.

Strategies for Longevity in the Trading Market

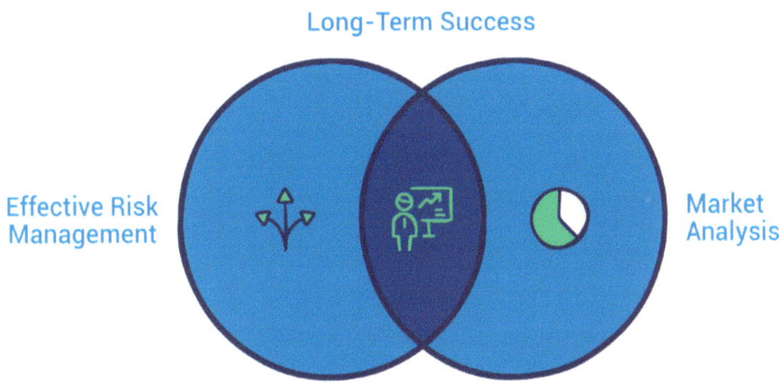

Notes

Notes

Notes

Notes

Notes

Notes

Notes

Notes

Notes

Notes

Monthly Review

Schedule a regular review of the investments to assess performance against expectations.

Month	
Assessment	

09

BUILDING A ROBUST TRADING THESIS

This section outlines a structured approach to developing and managing a trading thesis.It emphasizes the importance of stress testing the thesis, understanding market conditions, and employing effective position management strategies. Additionally, it highlights the significance of Bayesian inference in updating trade beliefs, defining ideal trade scenarios, and identifying sub-optimal trades. The guide aims to simplify the analysis process while ensuring thorough testing of data points, ultimately leading to more informed trading decisions.

Build Your Thesis

Stress Test the Thesis

- **Listen to Critics**
- **Recognize Cognitive Biases**
- **Market Conditions**
    - **Bear Market: To Buy, Fight Fear**
    - **Bull Market: To Sell, Fight Greed**

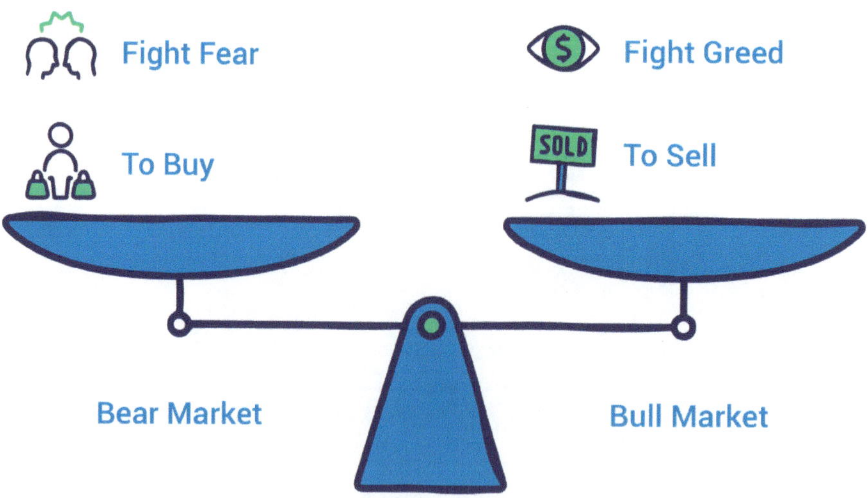

Strategies for Market Conditions

Position Management Strategy

- Put up one-third of Position
- Market Movement
    - Prices Climb Half as High as Expected: Take Final Position

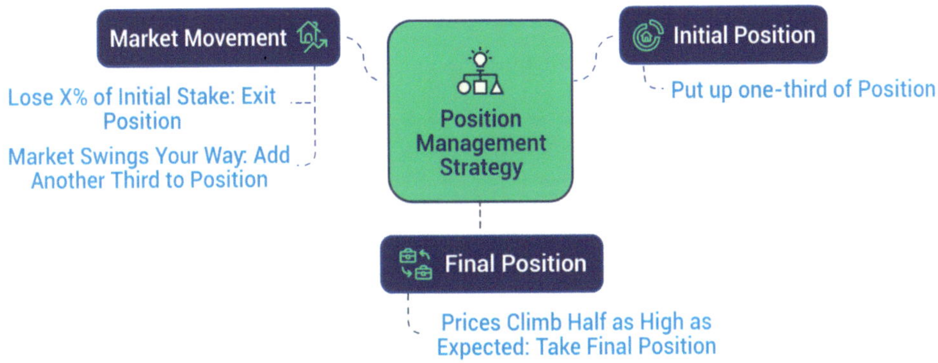

Bayesian Inference

Update Trade Beliefs with New Information

Define Ideal Trade Scenario

- What Do I Want to Happen in the Trade?
- Structure Trade to Maximize the Ideal Scenario

Trade Structuring Funnel

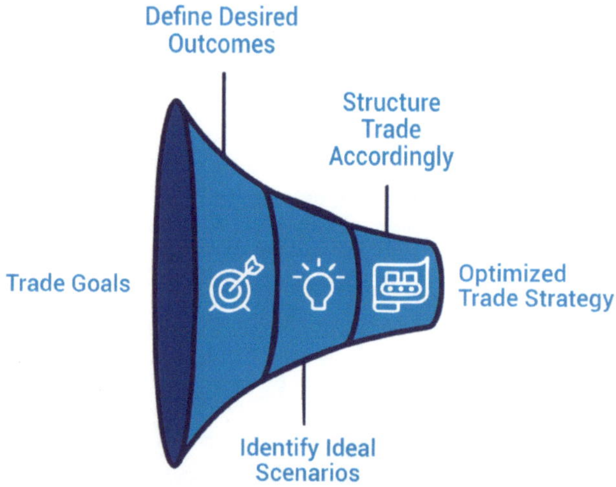

Identify Sub-Optimal Trades

- Look for Failure Points
    - Quickly Reduce Risk When Trade Goes Against Ideal Scenario

- Weekly Chart Not Confirming on Friday
- Retest of Breakout Not Immediately Bouncing
- No Immediate Continuation After Initial Entry
- Extreme Candles (Hammer, Inverted Hammer, etc.)
- Full Body Candles in Wrong Direction
- Blow-off Top/Bottom Action
- Intermarket Analysis Flags
    - Equity Does Not Rise with Its Index
    - Currency Does Not Weaken as Others Strengthen
    - Group of Related Commodities Strong While One Remains Weak

Focus on Simplified Analysis Funnel

- Avoid Overcomplicating with Excess Data
- Ensure Data Points Are Thoroughly Tested and Complementary
    - Conditional Edge Stacking for Conviction and Bet Sizing

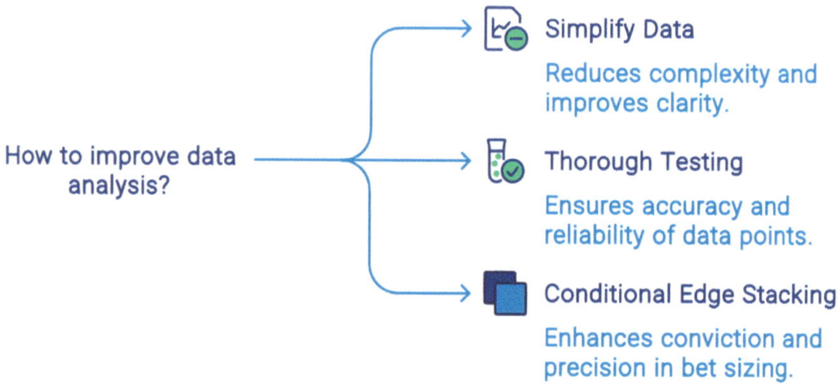

Avoid False Certainty

- Manage Uncertainty with Rough Odds and Probabilities
- Focus on Risks of Ruin and Tail Events

Strategies for Managing Uncertainty

Deepening Mastery through Focused Attention

- **Execute Analysis Ruthlessly**

Be Willing to Admit Uncertainty When Needed

This structured approach not only aids in building a solid trading thesis but also enhances the trader's ability to adapt to changing market conditions and make informed decisions. By focusing on simplification and rigorous analysis, traders can navigate the complexities of the market more effectively.

Navigate with Clarity

Notes

Notes

Notes

Notes

Notes

Notes

Notes

Notes

Notes

Monthly Review

Schedule a regular review of the investments to assess performance against expectations.

Month	
Assessment	

Quarterly Review

Schedule a regular review of the investments to assess performance against expectations.

Quarter	
Assessment	

10 COMPREHENSIVE TRADING STRATEGY FRAMEWORK

This document outlines a structured approach to developing a successful trading strategy. It emphasizes the importance of combining technical and fundamental analysis, incorporating risk management principles, utilizing advanced trading tools, and continuously refining one's trading approach. By following this framework, traders can enhance their decision-making processes and improve their overall trading performance.

Start with Clear Strategy

Combine Technical and Fundamental Analysis

- **Use Technical Indicators**
    - Moving Averages
    - Fibonacci Retracements
    - MACD
    - RSI
    - Support and Resistance Levels
- **Conduct Fundamental Analysis**
    - Study Economic Indicators
    - Examine News Events
    - Analyze Company Earnings Reports
    - Evaluate Supply and Demand Dynamics

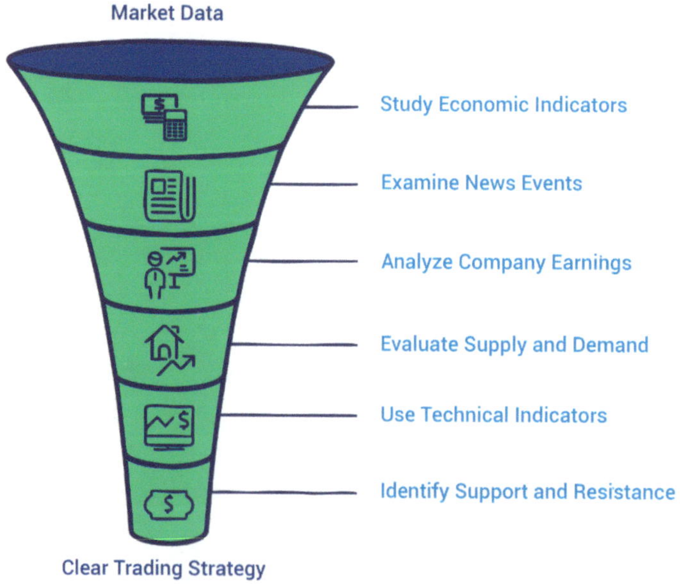

Incorporate Risk Management Principles

- Lack of Discipline
- Ignoring Risk Management
- Lack of Patience
- Emotional Trading
- Failure to Adapt to Market Conditions

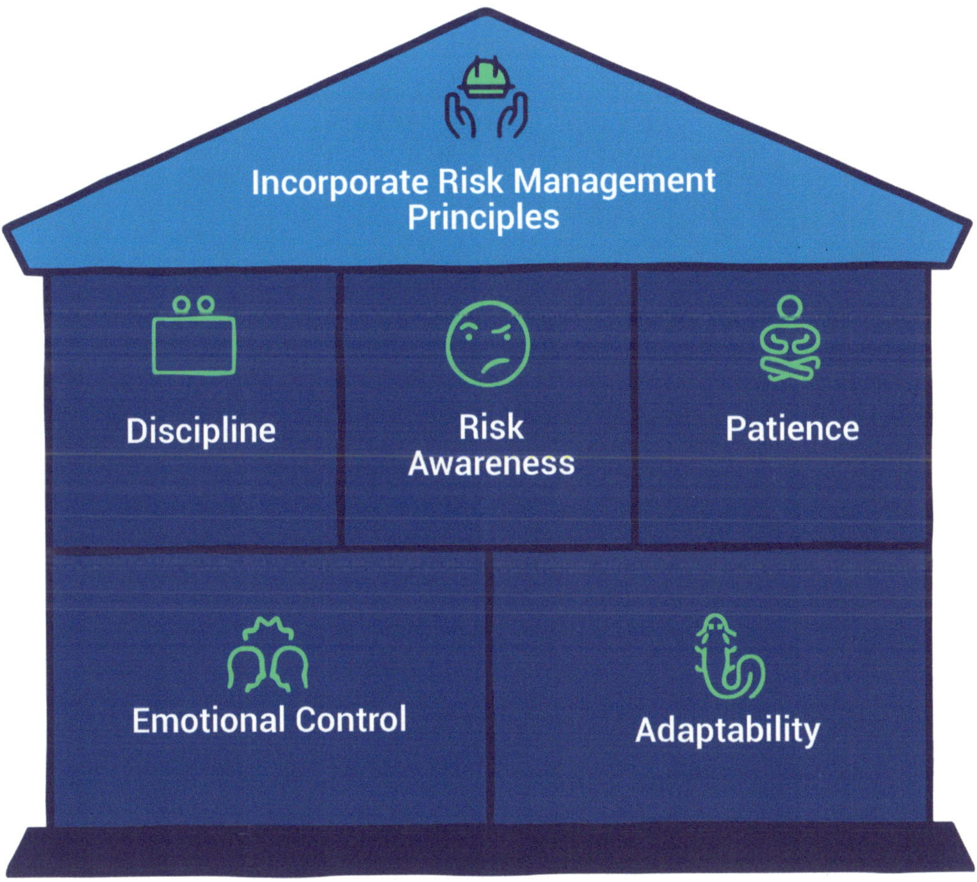

Use Advanced Trading Tools

- **Scalping Techniques**
  - Order Flow Analysis
  - Tick Charts
- **Automated Trading Systems**
  - Copy Trades from Professionals
  - Create Custom Algorithms

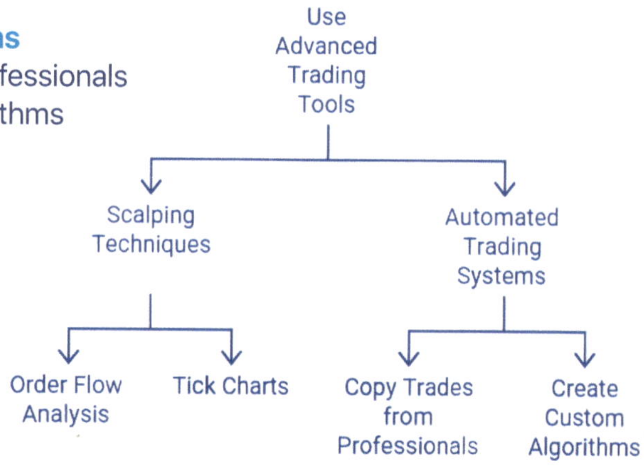

Identify High-Probability Trades

- **Swing Trading Approach**
  - Focus on Support and Resistance Levels
  - Analyze Trend Reversals
  - Study Chart Patterns

Swing Trading Cycle

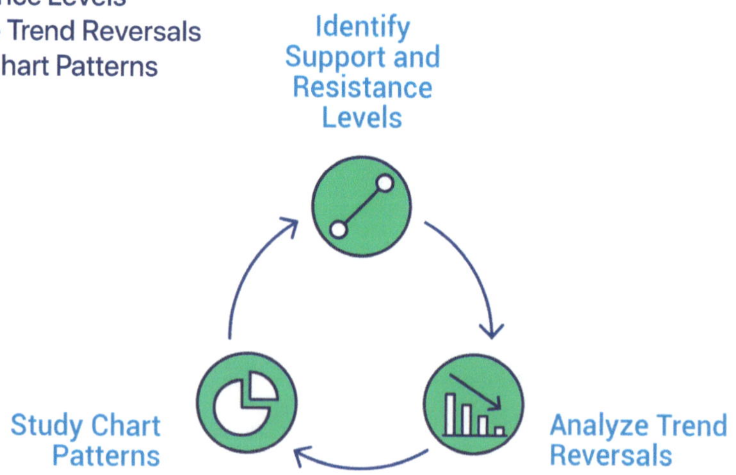

Risk Mitigation Strategies

- **Diversification Methods**
  - Spread Investments Across Different Assets
- **Hedging Techniques (If You Are a Sophisticated Investor)**
  - Use Derivatives like Options and Futures
- **Manage Market Volatility**
  - Use Stop-Loss Orders
    (Only You Can Determine Your Risk Tolerance)

Risk Management Strategies

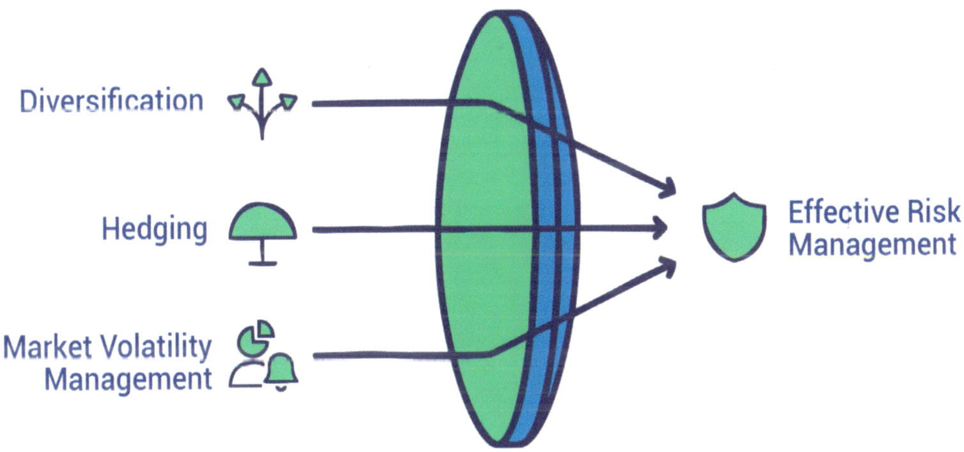

Fine-Tune Trading Approach

- **Continuous Learning and Improvement**
  - Read Books and Articles
  - Attend Workshops and Seminars
  - Network with Other Traders
- **Customize Trading Style**
  - Adapt Strategy to Changing Market Conditions

Trading Strategy Development

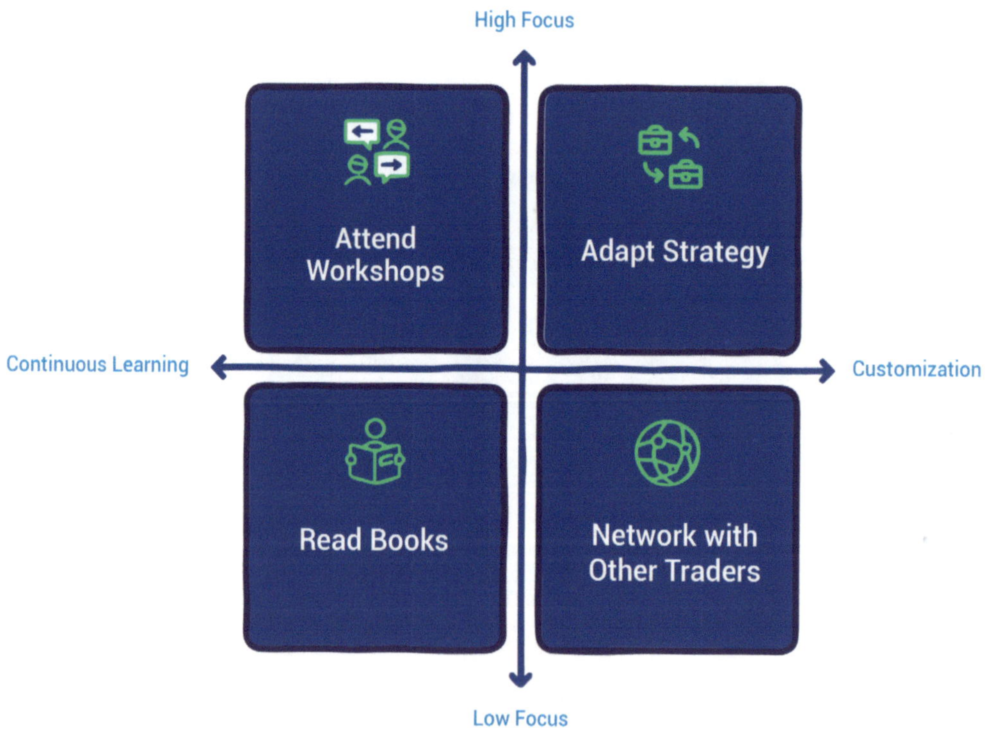

Conclusion

- **Risk Mitigation, Diversification, and Adaptability**
- **Take Control and Implement Ritchie's Strategy**
- **Transform Your Trading Style into a Masterpiece**

Elements Contributing to Mastering Trading

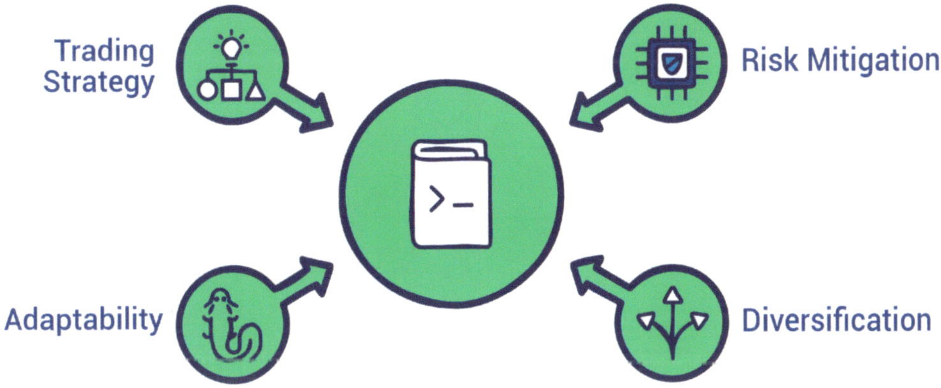

By adhering to this comprehensive framework, traders can navigate the complexities of the market with confidence and skill, ultimately leading to more successful trading outcomes.

Notes

Notes

Notes

Notes

Notes

Notes

Monthly Review

Schedule a regular review of the investments to assess performance against expectations.

Month	
Assessment	

11 STATISTICAL PERSPECTIVES ON TRADING INTERVENTIONS

This section explores the statistical implications of various trading interventions and their potential impact on your trading account. By understanding the trade-offs associated withholding or cutting trades, traders can make informed decisions that align with their risk-reward strategies. The insights provided here are grounded in statistical reasoning and Bayesian inference, allowing for a more nuanced approach to trading.

How to manage your trading account?

Hold trades

Minimize risk, maximize potential profit

Cut trades

Reduce losses, limit potential profit

Holding Losers

The more you hold onto losing trades and are lenient with them, the higher your win rate might become because you're giving the trade more time to work in your favor. However, this also increases the size of your average loser because you're not cutting the trade early, allowing it more time to turn further against you, possibly resulting in a full stop-out.

'olding losing trades increases average loss, stop-out risk

Holding Winners

Holding winners has the opposite effect. You might decrease your win rate because you're allowing the trade more time to potentially fall back against you. However, by doing so, you're also giving the trade more time to continue with the trend, which can increase the size of your average winner.

Cutting Winners Early

By cutting winners early, you increase your win rate since you're taking profits sooner. However, this action decreases the size of your average winner because you're not holding onto the trade for the larger gains that could come from bigger trends. This approach is more defensive, focusing on securing profits upfront.

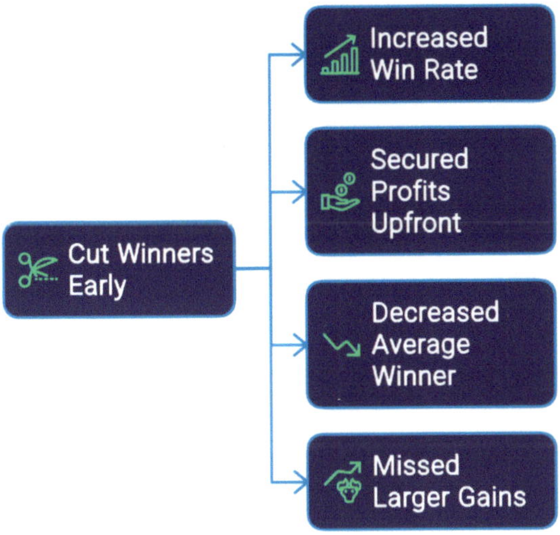

Cutting Losers Early

Cutting losers early, especially if you don't see follow-through in a trade, will decrease your win rate because you're not giving the trade as much time to work out. However, it also reduces the size of your average loser, potentially preventing full stop-outs. For instance, if a trade breaks out and goes sideways, cutting it early might result in smaller losses rather than letting the trade fully stop you out. Yet, some trades you cut early could eventually become winning trades.

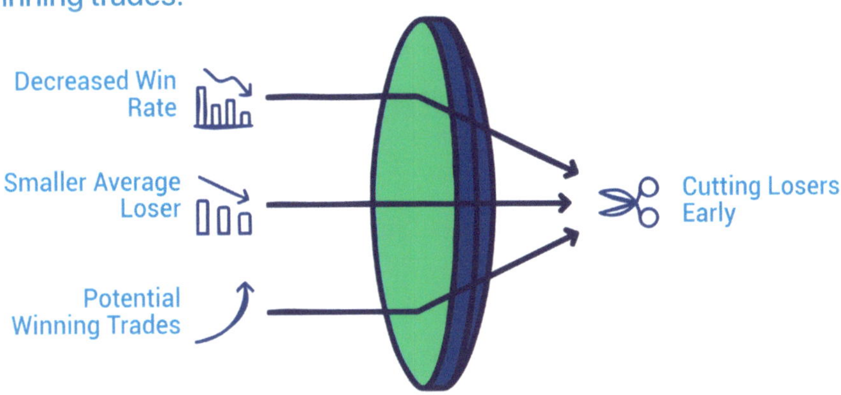

Conclusion

These are the trade-offs to keep in mind when making adjustments to a trade as it unfolds. Understanding the statistical implications of your trading decisions can help you navigate the complexities of the market more effectively, ultimately leading to better trading outcomes.

Every Step Matters: Trade Smart, Trade With Knowledge

Notes

Notes

Notes

Notes

Notes

Notes

Notes

Monthly Review

Schedule a regular review of the investments to assess performance against expectations.

Month	
Assessment	

12

ULTIMATE STOCK TRADE VALIDATION WORKSHEET

Trade Thesis

Investment Hypothesis

What is the fundamental idea or insight behind this trade?

Catalysts

What events or changes do you expect will drive the stock's movement?

Time Period

Over what period do you expect this thesis to play out?

Market Conditions

What are the current market conditions, and how do they support this thesis?

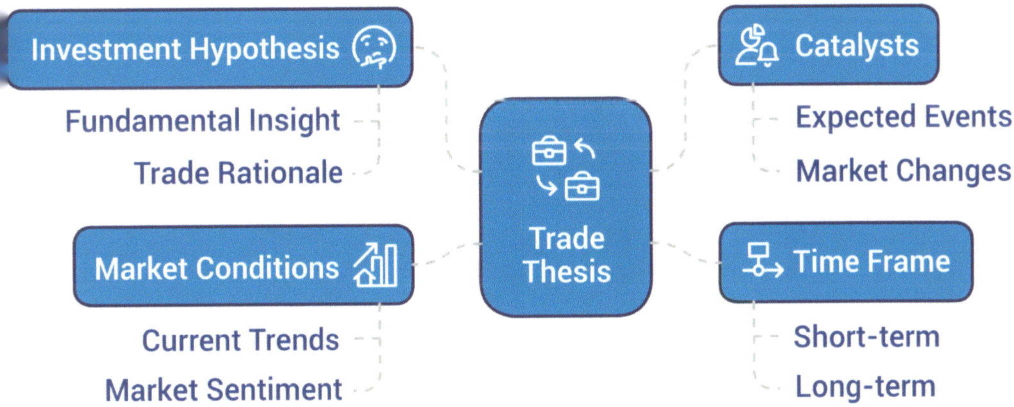

Trade Details

Stock Name/Ticker

Sector/Industry

Market (e.g., NYSE/NASDAQ)

Entry Period

Expected Holding Period

Step 1
Fundamental Analysis

1 Company Financial Health

Revenue Growth

Is the company's revenue consistently growing?

◯ Yes ◯ No

Supporting Data:

Earnings Growth

Is the company's earnings per share (EPS) increasing?

◯ Yes ◯ No

Supporting Data:

Profit Margins

Are profit margins stable or improving?

◯ Yes ◯ No

Supporting Data:

Company Financial Data

Overall Financial Health

2 Valuation Matrix

Price-to-Earnings (P/E) Ratio	
	Is the P/E ratio reasonable compared to peers/industry average? ◯ Yes ◯ No
	Current P/E Ratio:

Price-to-Book (P/B) Ratio	
	Is the P/B ratio favorable? ◯ Yes ◯ No
	Current P/B Ratio:

Price/Earnings-to-Growth (PEG) Ratio	
	Does the PEG ratio suggest fair value relative to growth? ◯ Yes ◯ No
	Current PEG Ratio:

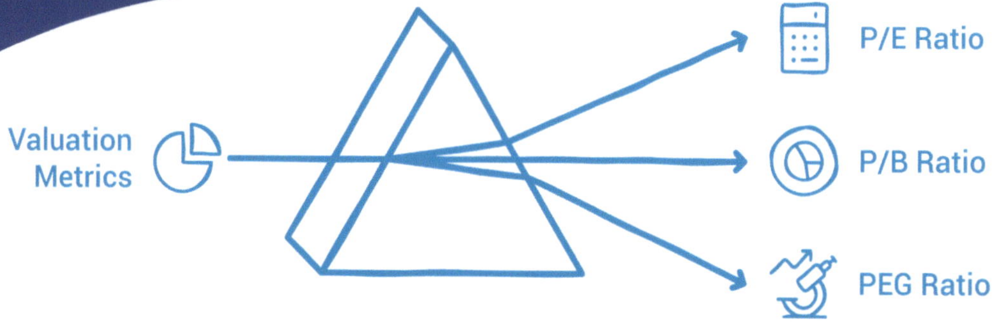

3 Dividend Yield (if applicable)

Dividend Yield

Is the dividend yield attractive?

◯ Yes ◯ No

Current Dividend Yield:

Dividend Stability

Is the dividend payout consistent and sustainable?

◯ Yes ◯ No

Supporting Data:

Dividend Evaluation

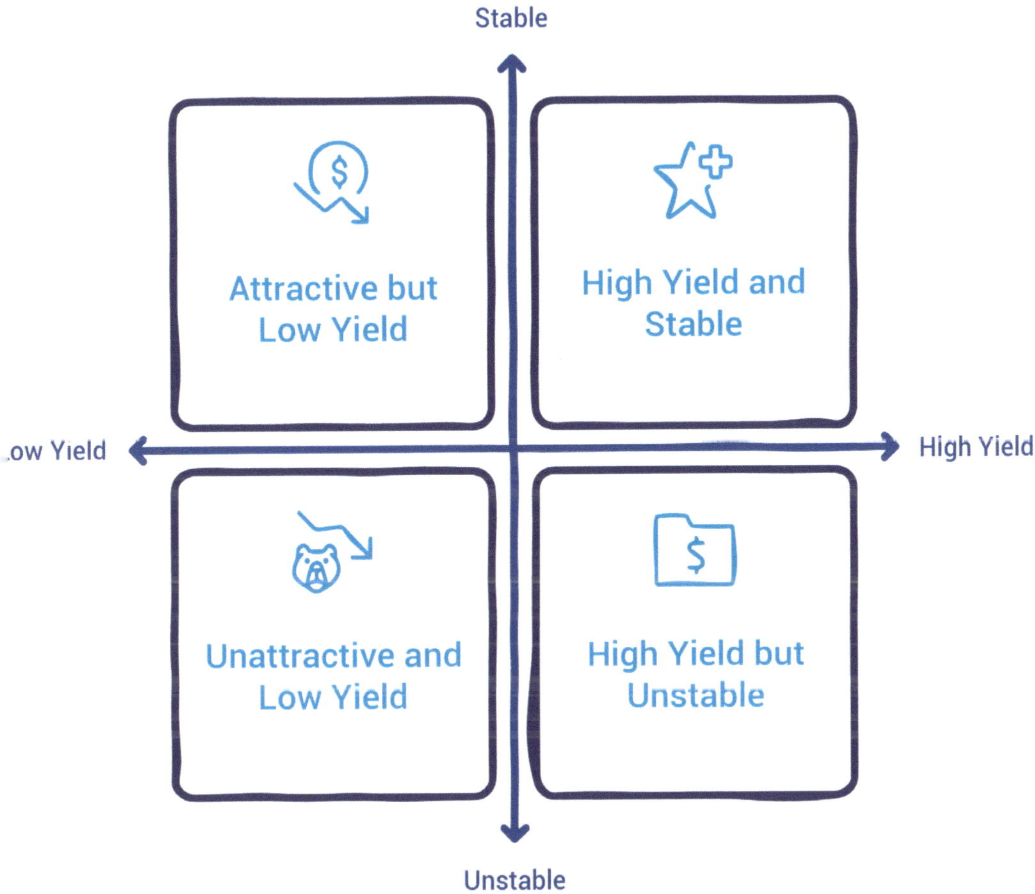

4 Economic and Industry Trends

Industry Growth

Is the industry growing?

◯ Yes ◯ No

Supporting Data:

Economic Indicators

Do macroeconomic indicators support growth in this sector?

◯ Yes ◯ No

Supporting Data:

Industry Growth

Supporting Data ←  → Economic Indicators

Overall Fundamental Analysis Conclusion

Step 2

Technical Analysis

1 Interest Rate Trends

What is the current trend of the stock?

VS

Upward Trend

Price is above key moving averages (MA 50 and MA 200)

Downward Trend

Price is below key moving averages (MA 50 and MA 200)

Current Trend (Up/Down/Sideways)

Key Moving Averages

Is the stock trading above/below key moving averages?

◯ Yes ◯ No

Supporting Data:

Support Levels

Support Levels

Resistance Levels

3 Volume Analysis

Volume Trends

Is there increasing volume supporting the trend?

◯ Yes ◯ No

Volume Data:

4 Momentum Indicators

RSI (Relative Strength Index)

Overbought/Oversold? ◯ Yes ◯ No

Current RSI:

MACD (Moving Average Convergence Divergence)	Are signals aligning with the trend? ◯ Yes ◯ No
	Current MACD:

Momentum Indicators Overview

MACD

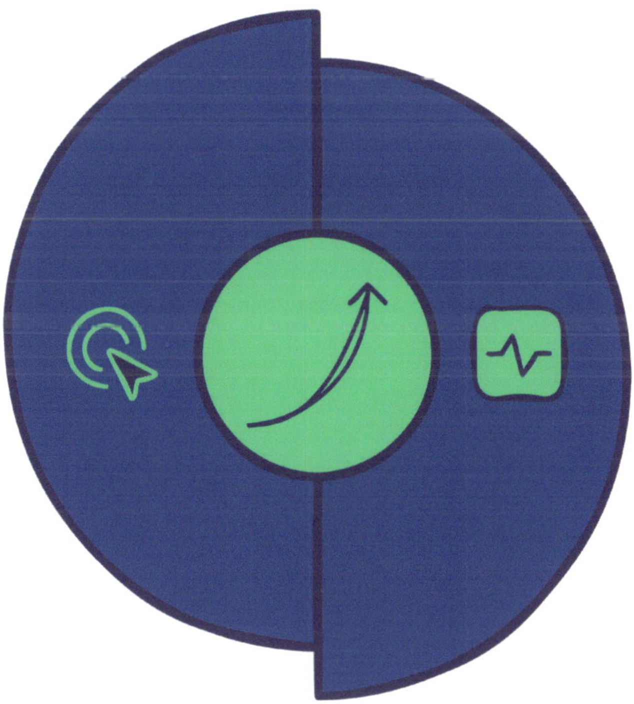

RSI

Chart Patterns

Are there any recognizable chart patterns (e.g., Head & Shoulders, Double Bottom, etc.)?

◯ Yes ◯ No

Identify Patterns:

Candlestick Patterns

Are there any significant candlestick patterns indicating a reversal or continuation?

◯ Yes ◯ No

Pattern Identified:

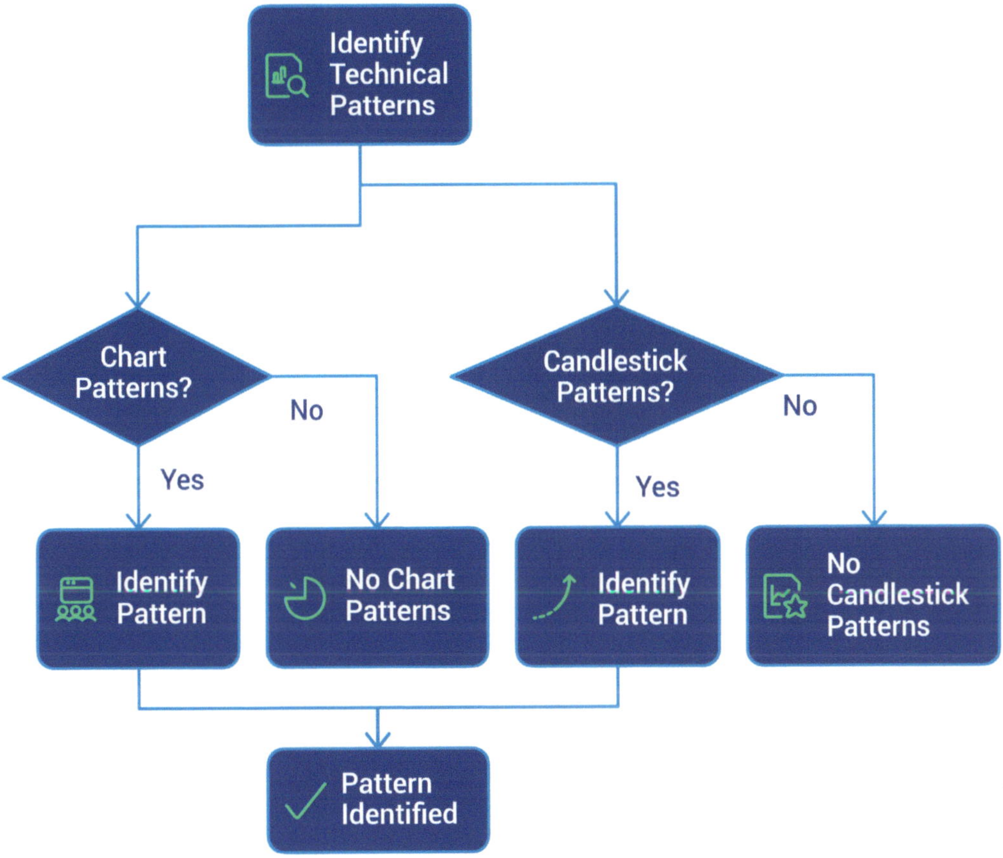
Identify Technical Patterns
Chart Patterns?
No
Yes
Candlestick Patterns?
No
Yes
Identify Pattern
No Chart Patterns
Identify Pattern
No Candlestick Patterns
Pattern Identified

Embrace the Future with Confidence

Overall Technical Analysis Conclusion

Step 3

Market Sentiment Analysis

1 News Sentiment

Overall Sentiment

Is the news/media sentiment regarding the stock positive?

◯ Yes ◯ No

Sources:

Analyst Ratings Consensus

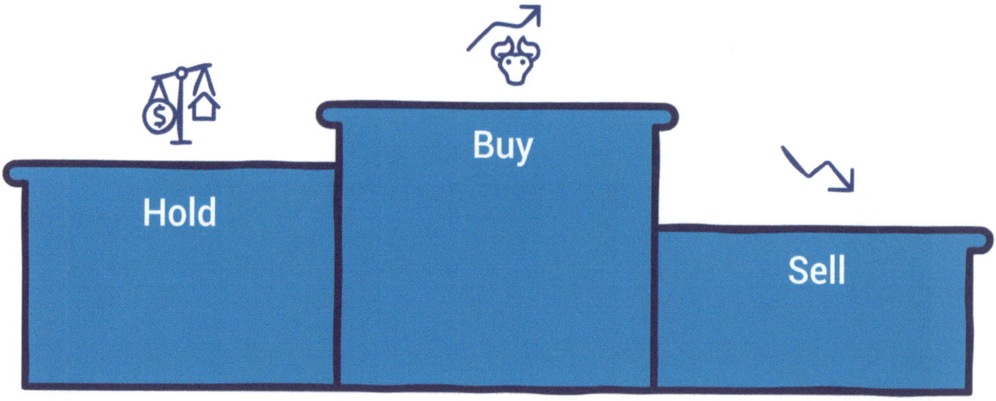

Latest Analyst Ratings

What is the consensus? ◯ Buy ◯ Hold ◯ Sell

Rating Agencies:

3 Investor Sentiment

Insider actions influence market sentiments

Insider Trading

Are insiders buying or selling shares? ◯ Yes ◯ No

Supporting Data:

Welcome Positive Energy!

Overall Market Sentiment Conclusion

Step 4 Macro-Economic and Global Factor

1 Interest Rate Trends

How will interest rate changes impact this stock or sector?

Positive

Increased investment opportunities, higher returns

VS

Negative

Decreased investment opportunities, lower returns

Impact of Interest Rates

How might current or anticipated interest rate changes impact this stock or sector?

◯ Positive ◯ Negative

Global Economic Factors

Currency Fluctuations ← → Trade Policies

Impact of Global Events

Are there global economic factors (e.g., trade policies, currency fluctuations) that could impact this stock?

◯ Yes ◯ No

Analysis:

3 Sector-Specific Macro Trends

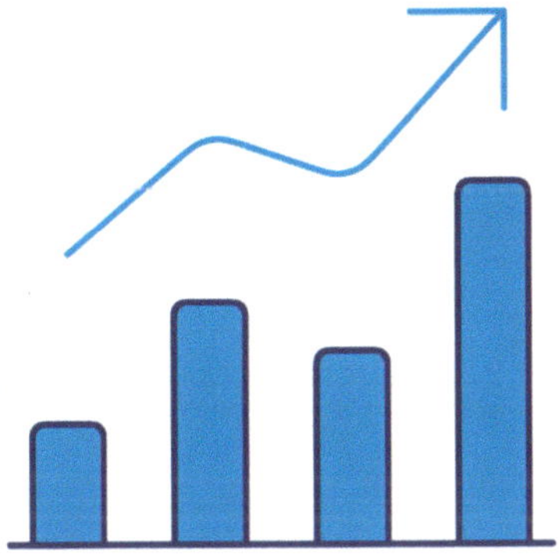

Navigating Sector Trends

Industry-Specific Trends

Are there any macroeconomic trends specifically affecting this sector?

◯ Yes ◯ No

Analysis:

Adapt to Transform our Outlook

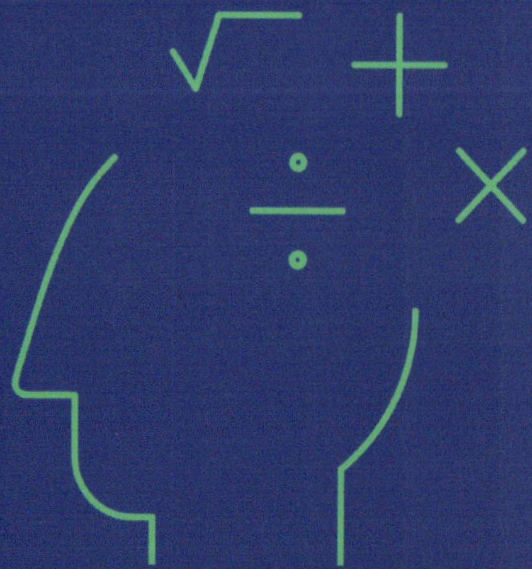

Overall Macro-Economic and Global Factors Conclusion

Step 5

Risk Management

1 Position Sizing

Capital Allocated:

Position Size:

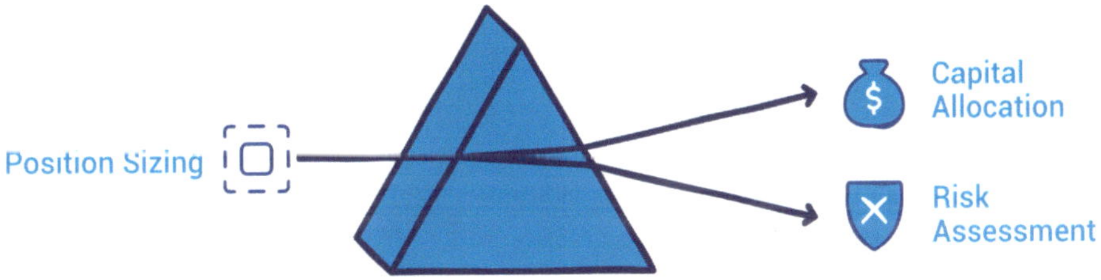

2 Stop-Loss Placement

Stop-Loss Level:

Risk per Trade (% of Capital):

Decision to Place Stop-Loss → Specify Stop-Loss Level → Calculate Risk per Trade → Express Risk as Percentage of Capital

3 Risk-Reward Ratio

Expected Reward:

Risk Reward Ratio (minimum 2:1):

Risk-Reward Ratio

Pros	VS	Cons
High potential reward		High risk
Justifiable risk		Uncertain outcomes

4 Alternative Scenarios

Best-Case Scenario

Potential Rewards:

Worst-Case Scenario

Potential Loss:

Neutral Scenario

Expected Outcome if the stock trades sideways:

Alternative Scenarios

Navigate the Path of Risk

Overall Risk Management Conclusion

Step 6

Psychological Readiness

1 Emotional Check

Is this trade influenced by emotion (e.g., fear of missing out, revenge trading)? ◯ Yes ◯ No

Confidence Level: ◯ High ◯ Medium ◯ Low

Emotional Check

fear of missing out

revenge trading

2 Plan Adherence

Does this trade fit within your overall trading plan and strategy? ◯ Yes ◯ No

Stay True to Your Strategy

Embrace the Journey Ahead

Overall Psychological Readiness Conclusion

Step 7

Trade Exit Strategy

1 Exit Conditions

Target Price:

Trailing Stop:

Fundamental Change:

2 Contingency Plans

If the trade doesn't go as planned, what contingency plans are in place (e.g., adjusting stop-loss levels, hedging)?

Navigate the Unexpected

Step 8

Ethical Considerations

1 Corporate Governance

Is the stock trading above/below key moving averages?

◯ Yes ◯ No

Supporting Data:

Ethical Issues

Environmental, Social, and Governance (ESG) Factors

2

Does the stock align with your personal or institutional ESG criteria?

◯ Yes ◯ No

Supporting Data:

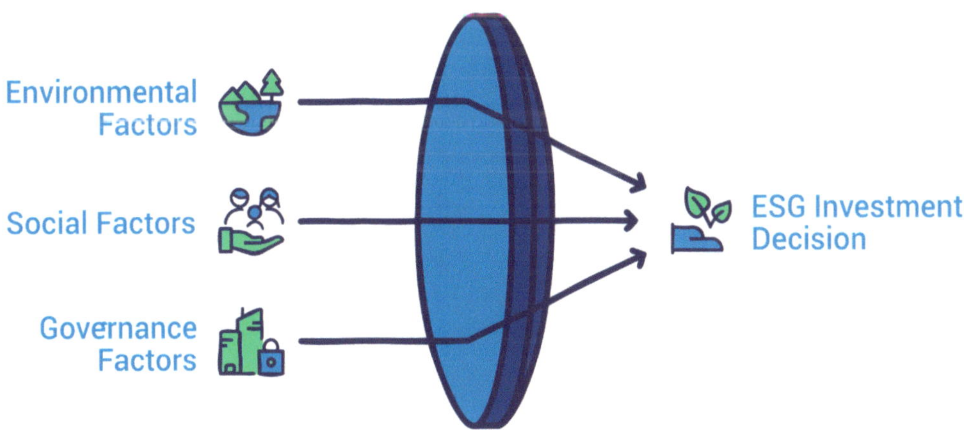

What are the overall ethical considerations of the project?

Positive

Promotes ethical practices and responsible development

VS

Negative

Raises ethical concerns and potential risks

Overall Ethical Considerations Conclusion

Step 9

Final Decision

Trade Validation

Do all criteria support initiating this trade?

◯ Yes ◯ No

If any criteria are negative, reconsider or revise the trade plan.

Action

Initiate Trade? ◯ Yes ◯ No

Reason for Trade/No Trade:

Trade Validation and Action Decision

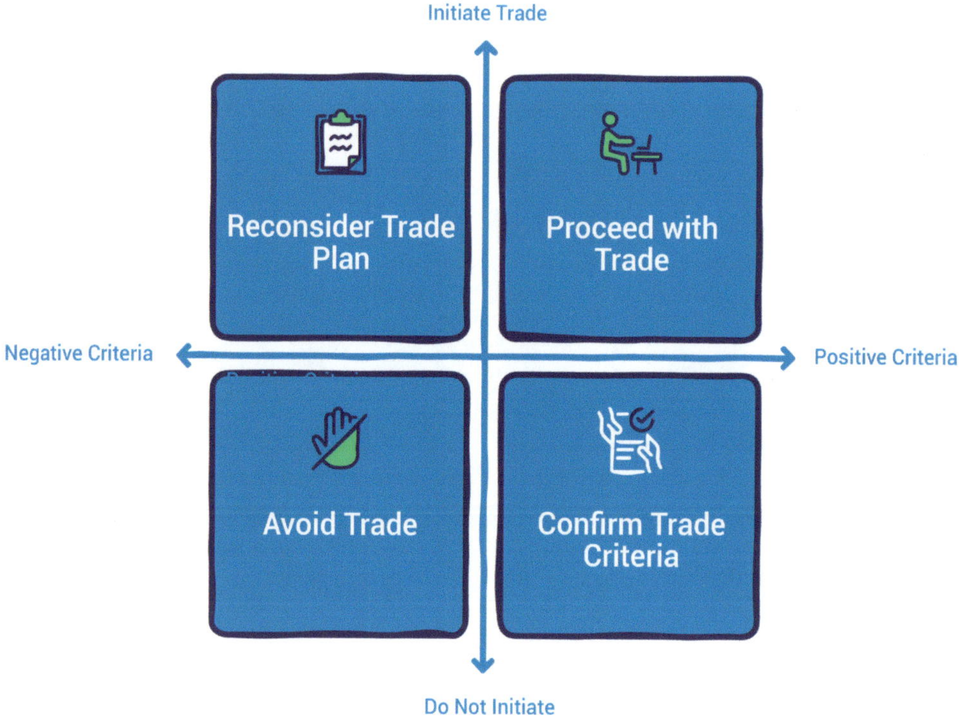

Post-Trade Analysis

Exit Date	

Outcome

Profit/Loss	Lessons Learned

Journal

Record a brief entry explaining the reasoning behind the trade and its outcome.

Notes

Notes

Notes

Notes

Notes

Notes

Notes

Monthly Review

Schedule a regular review of the investments to assess performance against expectations.

Month	
Assessment	

Quarterly Review

Schedule a regular review of the investments to assess performance against expectations.

Quarter	

Assessment

Yearly Review

Schedule a regular review of the investments to assess performance against expectations.

Year	
Assessment	

Trade Review Checklist

Use this checklist post-trade to evaluate what went right or wrong and document lessons learned.

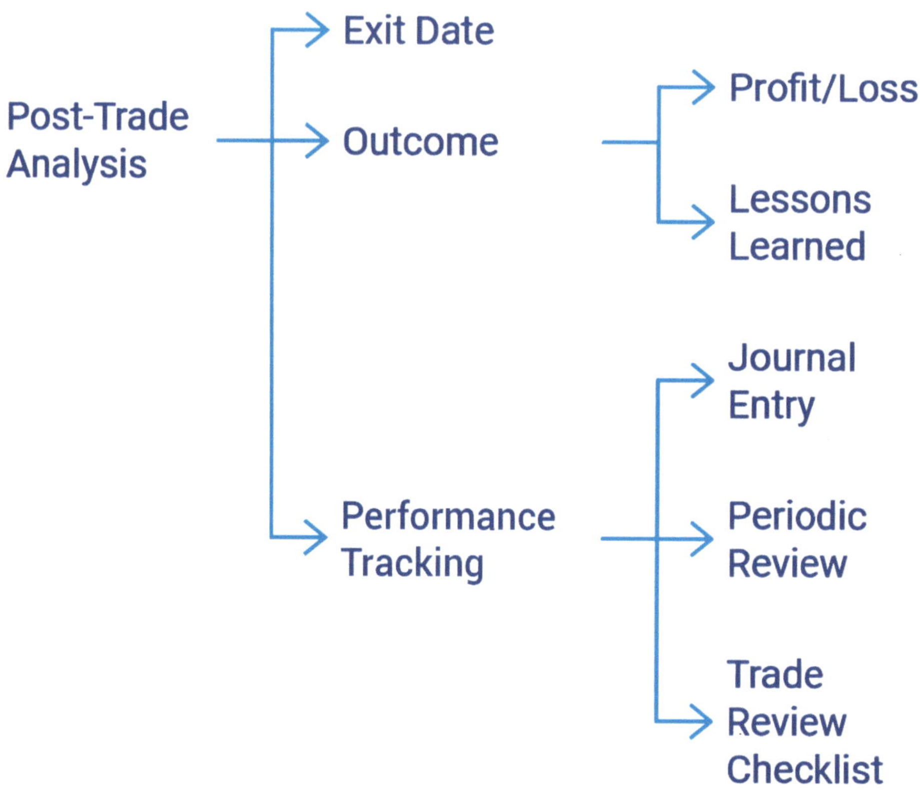
Post-Trade Analysis
Exit Date
Outcome
Profit/Loss
Lessons Learned
Performance Tracking
Journal Entry
Periodic Review
Trade Review Checklist

Notes

Notes

Notes

Notes

www.ingramcontent.com/pod-product-compliance
Lightning Source LLC
LaVergne TN
LVHW051154210926
848486LV00005B/275
9798892141208